"This book goes beyond self-help and good advice. It is based on unconditional love. It gives us creative activities that actually transform our lives."

Gerald G. Jampolsky, M.D.
Author of Love Is Letting Go Of Fear

"*Transformative Rituals* is a unique book. Its authors, David and Gay Williamson, have provided their readers with 25 exercises in personal transformation that they can use themselves, with their clients or with groups. Our society is myth-deprived, ceremony-deprived and ritual-deprived. This engaging book tries to redress this imbalance in a way that is *both inspirational and practical, both concrete and profound.*"

Stanley Krippner, Ph.D.
Professor of Psychology, Saybrook Institute
Co-author of Personal Mythology *and* Spiritual Dimensions Of Healing

"This book can help us survive our losses and make growth in the desired direction easier and more lasting."

Melba A. Colgrove, Ph.D.
Co-author of How To Survive The Loss Of A Love

"Rituals help us see the extraordinary in the ordinary, to celebrate what otherwise goes unmentioned, to close the door on the past or open to the future. The Williamsons provide a host of simple yet profound rituals for hallowing the whole of life. Our lives need them."

Walter Wink
Professor of Biblical Interpretation
Author of Engaging The Powers *and* Transforming Bible Study

"Rituals are a great part of our life. They express feelings that we have that would be beyond words to express. Human beings have used rituals as a means of meeting the most frightening, the most joyous moments of their lives probably ever since they have been humans. The Williamsons have done a great job of bringing ritual into 20th century life. Their book is original, imaginative, practical, transforming a very ancient way into a very modern way of meeting life's challenges and celebrating life's joys."

James Dillet Freeman
Poet & author of The Hilltop Heart

TRANSFORMATIVE RITUALS

TRANSFORMATIVE RITUALS
Celebrations For Personal Growth

Gay Williamson And David Williamson

Health Communications, Inc.
Deerfield Beach, Florida

Library of Congress Cataloging-in-Publication Data

Williamson, Gay
    Tranformative rituals: celebrations for personal growth/Gay Wil-
liamson and David Williamson.
      p.   cm.
    ISBN 1-55874-293-X (pbk.): $10.00
    1. New Age movement — Rituals — Texts. I. Rituals (Liturgical
books) — Texts. I. Williamson, David, 1934-. II. Title.
BP605.N48W555   1994   93-47040
264'.0993—dc20   CIP

Publisher: Health Communications, Inc.
               3201 S.W. 15th Street
               Deerfield Beach, Florida 33442-8190

Cover design and illustration by Andrea Perrine Brower

To David, my beloved partner, best friend and mentor — Your life is a continuing inspiration to me, and each day an unfolding experience.

To Gay — I love, honor and cherish you as author, life partner, mother, counselor and friend.

Transformative Ritual

I am power.
I am soul unfolding.
I am the lotus with petals of wisdom opening.
I am the sage and fire that cleanses.
I am the drum that beats in rhythm with the heart drum.

I am the resurrection.
I die to the old and celebrate the emergence of the new.
I honor the ancient wisdom of the ages.
I am the communion of all people.

I am the pain of love and the joy of sorrow.
I am honest, reflecting, risking and sharing.
I am the trust that opens and heals.
I am wholeness.

I am being, belonging and becoming in expression.
I am the journey to new places within.
I am the rite of passage to the voice of the heart's soul.
I am the sacred space of ritual, transformative ritual.

— *Gay Williamson*

Contents

Acknowledgments

We lovingly acknowledge our parents, Dave and Bernice Jackson and Dr.'s Maydene and Clinton Williamson, who instilled in us the spiritual life that is the foundation of this book. To Shirley and Bill Betzoldt and Mildred and Ed Woods who over a lifetime have shared their unconditional love and support. To Gay's sister, Lori Kesar, and husband Jeff who have shared their tenderness and laughter. To all of the Morgan family for the many years of family rituals and celebrations that took place in all our homes.

We especially love and appreciate our children Kyleigh, Josh, Keith, Kirk and Fred. Thank you for being our teachers. You have helped us grow in more ways than you will ever know, and it is a great privilege to be called your parents. We love and honor the uniqueness of each of you and love being a part of your process of unfoldment. A special thanks to Keith Williamson for sharing your talent as a graphic designer and spending hours creating graphics that complement these rituals.

A special appreciation to our loving friends who are our spiritual family at Detroit Unity Temple. We could never have done this without your prayers and willingness to join us on this spiritual path. Even when we said goodbye to one way of relating, we continued to be connected in a much greater realm as your spirits and stories are the heart of this book that we now share with the world. Our love goes to all the women who attended and experienced transformation in Gay's "Spirit Healer" retreats. Thanks to the people of Unity in Flint, Michigan; New York City; Richmond, California; Unity School of Christianity and the Association of Unity Churches where David served and developed experiences of holistic spirituality over three decades.

Special thanks to Dr. John Varani of the Center for Humanistic Studies in Detroit, and its founder Dr. Clark Moustakas. Your guidance, depth, educational process and counsel were the seeds of Gay's graduate research which led eventually to the writing and publishing of *Transformative Rituals*. David expresses appreciation to Dr. John Biersdorf and the Ecumenical Theological Center of Detroit where he studied, meditated and received his doctorate.

Special thanks to those who graciously gave permission to let us share their transformative ceremonies and stories. Special appreciation to our dear friend Dr. Tom Hopper, former Editor of *Wee Wisdom* magazine, for proofreading and making valuable suggestions. And for the hours of word processing and editing done by Michelle Gullet of Word Experts.

Without the championing and persistence of Barbara Nichols, editorial director of Health Communications, this book could not have been. Her spirit and love will always be deeply treasured.

How To Use This Book

In today's world, people hunger for meaning. We are starving for "soul" food, inner nourishment, a connection to our wellspring of spirituality, self-esteem and wellness. This book is about fulfilling those needs through rituals and ceremonies that connect us with our inner power and nourish us from within. Rituals are a vehicle to help us experience inner and outer transformation. Entered into in a highly conscious and meaningful way, rituals can enhance one's spirituality, provide an opening to a new sense of self-worth and bring about emotional healing during times of change.

In our extensive work, we have found that people crave transformative experience and this book provides specific steps to help facilitators take people on an inward, life-transforming journey. Included are some of our favorite rituals that we have used successfully in mainstream groups and with individuals in a number of different settings — recovery, counseling, spiritual, family and educational. Transformative is the word that best describes the intensity which flows from these rituals. We call them "Transformative Rituals," or TR for short.

Specific experiences are outlined to provide a recipe for rituals that can be used on a personal or professional level. Like all recipes, these can be adjusted to suit your own personal taste and style. Through TR, you can take your own personal journey inward or outward with others, in ways that are creative, nurturing and fulfilling. Here are some examples:

A middle-aged woman begins menopause. She invites the entire family to a special dinner in honor of her change of life. The positive energy generated from the experience gives her new vitality. She decides to retire from her current position and take on a new career in a field in which she has long been interested.

A minister performs a ritual which invites people to use their inner wisdom to allow a spiritual name to come to each of them. The name signifies a vision of each person's life and the ritual becomes an annual rite-of-passage into the new year.

A substance abuse counselor passes around a small, red, stuffed heart to people in her support group. The heart symbolizes a place where heart-felt feelings can be shared. The ritual allows participants to open themselves to others and tell their tales of struggle and triumph over adversity.

A patient reads a letter to God in an empowering therapy session. A new inner world of spirituality is opened up and a clearer vision of relationship to God is discovered.

These examples reflect a new paradigm for ritual. The movement is away from the rote ceremonies, traditionally performed only by clergy, toward rituals in which everyone reflects on their inner natures and share that with one another. Everyone shares power equally.

The purpose of the creative ceremonies we present and practice is not to "appease" or seek Divine favor, but to contact the power within us and share it with others in a sacred experience of common union. As you move confidently into self-realization and self-expansion through these rituals, you will come into your own empowerment and highest life expression.

There is a loving, creative spirit within each person that is universal and omnipresent, the creative life force. Through TR, we become aware of that which is sacred within us. As we share in these rituals together, our lives are profoundly changed and we experience a heightened awareness of soul, mind and body.

Transformative Rituals have their roots in our everyday experiences. When we pause to find the sacredness in the everyday context of life, we are renewed and transformed. To tap into the essence of the transforming power, we need to develop a kind of reverence for our inner world of images, symbols, metaphors, dreams and intuitive reflections. Ritual, images and symbols have been calling to us all, beckoning us to listen and learn and become.

Much of what is healing, harmonizing and empowering in ritual are the symbols that emerge. We are "symbolists," and our culture is full of symbols. Recently we saw a pair of black, high-top gym shoes with a famous perfume name and logo (symbol) written across the back. These ordinary shoes cost hundreds of dollars. Of course, the symbol is what people are willing to spend exorbitant amounts of money to display. Designer dresses, jeans, sunglasses, cars and sports equipment are marketed as symbols of success, status, power, prestige, popularity, sensuality and belonging.

Putting on gym shoes that cost hundreds of dollars may give a person a temporary feeling of power or belonging, but unless we get beyond these outer things and to our *authentic* power, creativity and sense of being, we will always be chasing after the next status symbol, caught up in the devastating trap of consumerism. We may sacrifice precious time with our family and friends in order to earn enough to buy these things — some young people even resort to murder to get the gym shoes or signature jacket they feel they must have. Consumerism can become compulsive as we search for things outside of us to make us feel okay. Perhaps this strong programming to "get it and be happy" sets us up unconsciously to mood-alter with food, alcohol, drugs and other sources for the "fix" to "feel good."

Our misguided search for meaning in life too often leads to consumerism, which is devastating our planet at an alarming rate. And like our planet, we are left empty. We can get caught up in the work-to-consume cycle again and again by rewarding ourselves with another trinket from the mall — after all, we have worked so hard, we deserve some symbol of recognition. The symbol, on a superficial level, has a temporary feel-good effect, but there is a high price to pay.

We need to stop and ask ourselves: What is the desire behind having that symbol or item? Is it that I desire to feel a certain way? Is there a part of me that needs to be recognized, and I think the symbol will give me that attention or recognition? How can I recognize my inner needs? How can I connect with my own inner wisdom and appreciate my innate power and authority? How can I honor and appreciate the power of my own life myth? My own uniqueness and the special gifts I bring to the world? How can I move into the experience of feeling bonded, connected and satisfied within my own family, community and world?

The need to be in touch with our own life meaning through the symbolic life was expressed by the noted Swiss psychologist, Carl Jung. Jung asks:

> Where do we live symbolically? Nowhere, except where we participate in the ritual of life. But, who, among the many, are really participating in the ritual of life? Very few . . .

Have you got a corner somewhere in your house where you perform the rites, as you can see in India? Even the very simple houses there have at least a curtained corner where the members of the household can lead the symbolic life, where they can make their new vows or meditation. We don't have it; we have no such corner. We have our own rooms, of course — but there is a telephone which can ring us up at any time, and we must always be ready. We have no time, no place . . .

Only the symbolic life can express the need of the soul — the daily need of the soul, mind you! And because people have no such thing, they can never step out of this mill — this awful, grinding, banal life in which they are "nothing but . . ." These things go pretty deep, and no wonder people get neurotic. Life is too rational; there is no symbolic existence in which I am fulfilling my role, my role as one of the actors in the divine drama of life.

Today, we need symbols that emerge from our inner experiences that are evoked in rituals, ceremonies and rites-of-passage. Each of us may have encoded within our own structure the symbols for our wholeness — probably in our DNA. Everything around us in nature and the animal kingdom points to our innate wisdom, creativity and healing power. It is our journey to unlock these symbols from within ourselves and to re-enact them in ritual. From the shifting in our conscious awareness we are healed, we are guided, we live fulfilling lives and we feel connected in a dynamic way to others around us. When we feel connected to the larger fabric of life, it affects us all, and together we are healed from that sense of isolation and loneliness. Eventually, as we come together in the space of ritual and ceremony, we are brought closer to ourselves and to each other. As Jung told us, our souls need nourishing daily, our inner worlds need our acknowledgment regularly.

We all have great moments when we celebrate births, weddings, funerals, bar/bas mitzvahs, graduations, confirmations and other events. Sometimes these rites-of-passage and rituals are five, ten or twenty years apart. What do we do with all those years between? There are many opportunities to create ways to honor the sacred in our everyday experience, to bring the symbols and metaphors of our own story forth from within and celebrate them together.

Rituals help us connect to a flow of energy within that can transform who we are and what we can become. From the recesses of our own minds, symbols arise that give us meaning and purpose, that energize our lives while healing us at our deepest levels. We create a harmony and begin to resonate with others and feel the most intimate sense of being a part of others' lives. We connect to images and memories from our ancestry that can heal our families and communities. Ancient wisdom and hidden streams of life are revealed as we open to our future with conscious use of creative ritual and inner symbols.

We share TR with love, and hope to bring much joy, satisfaction and miraculous transformation to each person joining in these unique adventures.

1

Burning Bowl Ceremony

Part of the experience of living involves making mistakes. No one can say with certainty that they have not done anything in their lives that they do not regret. There is always some aspect of ourselves that we would like to change, that we would like to cleanse from our consciousness. But sometimes, the unwanted image of ourselves is hard to get rid of in our mind's eye. If we cannot clear this image, then change is difficult. The Burning Bowl Ceremony is a symbolic way to cleanse our lives, to rid ourselves of the old pictures in our heads and replace them with a new way of viewing ourselves and our world.

YOU'LL NEED

Lightweight paper, such as onion skin (there is less smoke from this type of paper); pens or pencils; a wok or other metal pan with a sturdy base or stand; a screen to cover the top of the wok to prevent ashes from escaping; Sterno or some other means of lighting the paper, such as a candle in a stand; and a fire extinguisher for safety.

THE RITUAL

Give each person a small piece of paper and something to write with. Some people may want to burn entire diaries or come with volumes of material. Encourage them to complete a brief synopsis of what they want to cleanse and release from their lives.

Begin a meditation like this:

The Burning Bowl Ceremony is a symbolic way to cleanse our lives, to let go of the mistakes and failures of the past and move on. The fire in the Burning Bowl is a symbol of transformation. The fire takes the paper and changes it from one form to another. Likewise in our lives we will take these blocks, fears, old hurts, mistakes and burn them. This releases our personal power, freeing it up to work in our lives in a more constructive way. We realize it takes a lot of energy to keep mistakes and fears hidden. Now it is time to let them go. Now is the time to take that energy and choose to use it in a way that is conscious and life enhancing. Begin to allow some of the things you want to let go of in your life to come to your mind.

As we approach the end of this meditation, we will have the opportunity to write some of these things down on our paper. Let them come to you in an easy way now, not trying to force or make them up. Just let them come to you, and as they do, slowly open your eyes and write them on your paper. You may want to start your writing with "I am free from . . ." Take some time and write, then close your eyes again and let another thought come to you and write it down. Take as much time as you need. Today is a new and fresh day. Today we are new people, meeting life in a new way.

Have people come up one at a time or form a line, depending on the size of your group. Ignite their papers and put them in the Burning Bowl. During this process, music, singing or other readings can be performed while people place their papers into the flames. Sitting in silence is also all right.

After the Burning Bowl is completed, a "Letter To God" or "Letter to Higher Power," as described in Chapter Five, can close the experience.

> Note: *It is suggested that someone attend the Burning Bowl at all times to assure safety while papers are burning. Do not put the Burning Bowl on carpet or other flammable material.*

TRANSFORMATION STORY (FROM GAY)
I used the Burning Bowl Ceremony in a substance abuse

therapy group. A member of the group, an attorney named Reuben, had not been able to maintain his sobriety even after a long period of abstinence.

Reuben had lost touch with his emotions and told the group, "I often find out what I am feeling by analyzing my actions, trying to determine what they might feel like. I rarely feel emotions directly." Reuben continued, "I say I must be feeling this way because I am acting such and such a way."

One day, I introduced Reuben and the group to the Burning Bowl Ceremony. Following the ritual, I passed out a little box filled with "Angel® Cards." On each card was written an insight, positive adjective or state of being.

Reuben pulled a card that read "creativity." He said he had wanted to get back into creative writing and poetry. I suggested that he write a poem about the Burning Bowl experience. The poem Reuben composed spoke of his struggle with addiction and the pain he had buried for a long time. Here is Reuben's poem, an example of the inner transformation that takes place in ritual:

The Burning Bowl

I've been playing the game for many years
Sitting shoulder to shoulder at the bar
With the other players, as the hands are dealt
To us in the smoky room, wrapped in glass.

At first I would win a pot or two
Raking in some smiles, laughter and fun.
The Dealer grinned and poured me another card.
He was patient because he worked for the house
And he knew the house can never lose.

As the cards got worse I held my hand
Closer to my heart so others could not see,
While I bet pieces of my soul and
The tears of those I loved on losing hands.

Other players would win a pot or two
And I would envy their brief bit of joy.
And bet more of my life on a hopeless bluff.
But the game was no longer one of chance,
The odds had flown and there was but one end.

Then I was told, "You cannot win the game
But through God you no longer have to play."
So I brought my losing cards from my heart.
And let others see the weak hand I held
Upon which I had wagered and lost so much.
Before the honest flame of their caring hearts
My precious cards twisted into the black
And brittle shapes they had always been.

When Reuben read the poem to the group, his emotions totally caught him by surprise. For the first time, he participated in his feelings and choked up with emotion as he realized the pain of his addiction. It was like seeing the "ice man" thaw before our very eyes. Everyone in the group was deeply touched. The last time I saw Reuben he was continuing successfully in his recovery, learning every day about living with his feelings.

As demonstrated in the story of Reuben, rituals in recovery set the pace for a new lifestyle. Drug and alcohol use is a ritual. One director of a residential treatment center suggests: "I think people come in here and they have a lot of drug pattern rituals. What we do is try to get them to think about rituals of recovery. Rituals provide order, meaning and purpose to life. Drug rituals provide meaning and purpose in life as well, but eventually they will either kill a person or create sickness and disease."

Many of the TR experiences can be adapted and work extremely well in establishing the pace for a happier, fulfilling, drug-free lifestyle.

WHO CAN USE THE RITUAL

Individuals . . . A person can use this to let go of limiting thoughts, fear, lethargy, past mistakes, hostility, desperation and self-doubt.

Families . . . Members of a family could join in together in a personal ritual of closure and a new beginning. The TR can be used at significant times in a family's life or periodically to clear out hurt feelings and anger.

Therapists . . . Can help clients let go of blame, self-criticism, stressful thoughts and behaviors, hurt, anger or anything that takes away from building a sense of self-worth and self-esteem.

Spiritual Leaders . . . Will help parishioners let go of a sense of separation from God and release fear, shame and lack of faith. The ritual can be incorporated into a Lenten series of Sunday lessons on forgiveness culminating with a Forgiveness Burning Bowl in which congregants symbolically forgive people, organizations or events in their lives that caused them hurt or harm.

Recovery Groups . . . May be used to help those in recovery let go of alcohol, drugs, self-abuse, hurts of the past and unforgivingness of self and others.

2
Heart-To-Heart Ritual

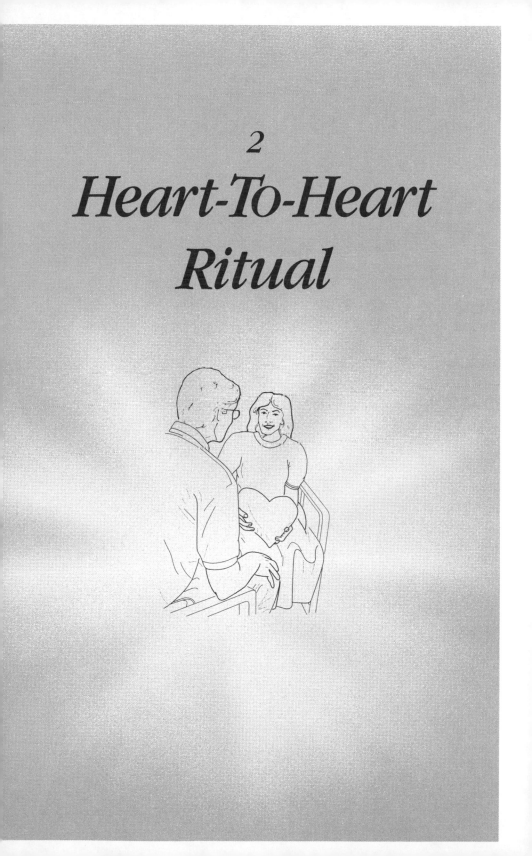

Open, honest communication is key to a healthy relationship — be it with a family member, a friend or a love interest. For many reasons — such as unassertiveness or not wanting to hurt others — people sometimes stuff their true feelings deep inside. This is dangerous because the feelings build up until they reach a boiling-over point and explode, sometimes hostilely. On the other side of the coin, people often don't listen carefully to their friends, relatives or partners when they are expressing their feelings. This can lead to resentment. Good communication must be two-way: speaking and listening openly and honestly.

The Heart-To-Heart Ritual was developed to facilitate better two-way communication. A symbolic heart is used to remind us to speak sincerely and listen attentively. Listening and speaking from the heart is an incredibly healing experience.

YOU'LL NEED

One stuffed heart or some other heart-shaped object or symbol.

THE RITUAL

The Heart-To-Heart Ritual can either be planned or spontaneous, and can be initiated by just one person. Everyone should come into the Heart-To-Heart Ritual with an open mind and a heart full of love and compassion.

People should be seated fairly close together in a circle. The environment should be quiet and free from distractions. Read the following Heart-To-Heart Commitment:

Heart-To-Heart
Commitment

I commit myself to speak from my heart all during this time of sharing. I agree to be honest with myself and others. I also will make every effort to listen intently, looking directly at the person with the heart who is speaking. I will help to create an atmosphere of trust, safety and peace where we can feel secure in reaching our own hearts and communicating Heart-to-Heart. I will honor and keep confident all that is shared and never use it against the person or as gossip later.

I make this commitment in the belief that love is the greatest thing in the world and can heal, uplift, harmonize, prosper and bring peace. I claim all of these good qualities and results for myself and others having a Heart-to-Heart with me.

The agreement can be modified to better suit your group's needs. Make sure that everyone understands and accepts it before you begin.

It is helpful to start your Heart-To-Heart Ritual with some sort of centering exercise — holding hands, sitting in silence for a few moments or whatever seems appropriate to focus people's thoughts. Begin by handing the heart to one of the participants. Only the person with the heart is allowed to speak. All others should listen with love and give that person their full attention. The person speaking can share whatever feelings come to mind. The purpose is to maximize expression of feelings, not to give a chronological rundown of current life events.

As each person finishes what he has to say, the heart is passed around the circle. The next person should express her feelings and not comment about, judge or analyze what anyone else in the group has said. The keys to the Heart-To Heart Ritual's success are honest expression and undivided attention.

The heart continues around the circle as many times as necessary. When no one has anything more to say, the Heart-To-Heart Ritual is concluded. The sharing can close with hugs or whatever seems to work best for the group.

TRANSFORMATION STORY

One evening our daughter, Kyleigh, who was about six years old at the time, called for a Heart-To-Heart. We gathered around the dining table with Kyleigh and our son, Joshua.

The children attended the same school and often Kyleigh would stand by Josh when he was lined up with his class. Josh, being three years older than Kyleigh, did not think it was acceptable having his little sister hanging around him and his friends.

As Kyleigh began the Heart-To-Heart she said, "Josh, the reason I come over and stand by you at school is because I miss you and I just want to be next to you because I love you."

Tears welled in all our eyes as we listened to the simple way Kyleigh had reached in and shared from deep in her heart the feelings she held for Josh. For the first time, Josh really heard the tender, heart-felt feelings Kyleigh was sharing. Ordinarily, he would have challenged her and justified why he didn't want her around. But because she had the heart, he had to listen. As she spoke, his heart was transformed and touched by her love. Today they couldn't be more loving and caring toward each other. They have developed the skill of listening from the heart. They still have their times of confrontation, but beneath that is a firm foundation of love, security and acceptance.

WHO CAN USE THE RITUAL

Families . . . Anyone in our home can ask for a Heart-To-Heart. Our children know they are able to convene the family when they need support or feel it necessary to work out a family problem. It also provides us with a structure for learning to really listen to one another. This ritual has truly enhanced our family relationships.

Therapists . . . The Heart-To-Heart Ritual is a great way to facilitate communication of feelings in a group setting. It can also provide skills for families or couples in counseling to begin heart-felt communication with each other. Additionally, couples can use the Heart-To-Heart Ritual in the evenings a few times a week as homework to increase intimate sharing and communication.

Spiritual Leaders . . . Use the Heart-To-Heart Ritual as a way to share prayer requests. At our church's annual prayer breakfast, we ask people to write out their prayer requests for themselves and others. Congregants sit at round tables with a heart placed at the center. Each table has its own Heart-To-Heart Ritual and members share their prayer requests. This gives people the experience of being supported in prayer by a spiritual community. It also allows people to get to know one another better. The Heart-To-Heart ritual can also be used at spiritual retreats; it helps to integrate the experiences of the retreat.

Recovery Groups . . . Heart-To-Heart rituals can be successfully used as a group process for working through substance abuse. They provide the opportunity for people to express what is really in their hearts and to be supported by others. The experience can be so validating that it encourages a new openness and honesty, both with others and one's self.

Teachers . . . Heart-To-Hearts help children appreciate the importance of respect, honor and keeping agreements. They also learn the importance of keeping private what is shared. The teacher may begin with sharing a fictitious story to illustrate the point, and follow with group discussion. This story and discussion can be made appropriate for each grade level. Heart-To-Hearts can also be used in college classrooms.

3
Life Symbol Ritual

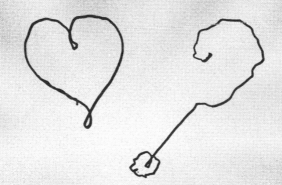

No two individuals are completely alike. We are complex beings with unique personalities and talents. It is easy to lose sight of the fact that we are special and here to fulfill a purpose, to add to the world in a distinct way. Sometimes we might even question our existence but, deep inside, we know who we are and what our purpose is. We just need to explore different, creative pathways to self-discovery. The purpose of the Life Symbol Ritual is to provide a better understanding of one's own meaning, purpose and individuality. It can also be an effective way for people to get to know one another.

YOU'LL NEED

A two-foot piece of flexible wire for each person; pliers; scissors; and pieces of ribbon.

THE RITUAL

Give each person a piece of wire. As they hold the wire in their hands, ask them to think about their lives. What does life in general mean to them? How do they feel about their lives now?

Lead them in a meditation or time of inner reflection like this:

Each of our lives is important. Each of us is a unique, special individual. Each of us has a special gift that we are to give the world — a gift that only we can give.

Think about your life and what it means. What is going on? What do you desire. What do you hope for? Think about the joy and sorrow you have experienced. You are a significant person, a divinity, a richness, a life-energy. You are a living soul. From the creation of the universe, through eons of evolution, you have appeared here at this place. You have your own memories, loves and fears. You have your own way of seeing and feeling things. You have the strength of decision and assent. You have a center of existence.

Sometimes you want to be like a sparrow — just another unrecognizable bird in the flock — that flies when and where the flock flies. The flock's collective conscience is the conscience you want to use. You want to see and feel what the flock does. You deny your ability to see and feel your own way.

You're not sure that you want to allow the "real" you to surface. But you have to be you. You cannot be anyone other than yourself.

So let's discover something more of what it means to *be ourselves.*

Take the wire in your hands. Relax, and let your creative energies surface — don't worry about being artistic. There is no right or wrong way to do this — just your way. Work the wire into a form, a symbol or a shape which represents you and your life. Don't try to design something nice or interesting. Let the shape come to you from within. Just quietly reflect and let it come. Let the wire move in your hands into a symbol of *your* life. It can be a sun, an arrow, a peace symbol — anything that represents you and your life.

Feel free to use all of the materials provided. Be as creative as you like — this is an expression of your life!

Find a secluded space to work if you need to. Please work in silence so we can all listen to our inner voices.

When everyone has finished, ask people to introduce themselves and share what their symbol means to them. So that everyone has the opportunity to share, have larger groups break up into mini-groups of about four people and follow the same procedure. Facilitators can form a wire of their own if they wish and join one of the mini-groups. When everyone has finished, form one large circle and share what some of the symbols are. Try to get around to as many people as possible, without letting anyone talk too long. Share your own symbol with the group.

WHO CAN USE THE RITUAL

Individuals . . . People seeking to understand more of their own meaning and purpose in life will gain a great deal from this TR. It can provide guidance and direction in fulfilling one's unique mission in life.

Therapists . . . The Life Symbol Ritual, shared in groups, can provide a way for people to introduce themselves and enter into group sharing. It also is a good creative experience for those who prefer to communicate in symbols. The ritual can provide insight into oneself and others.

Spiritual Leaders . . . The Life Symbol can be used as a way to allow Spirit to enter one's life more fully and prepare people for spiritual guidance and insight.

Recovery Groups . . . Those in recovery can use this powerful ritual to develop a symbol for their recovery. Many people who have participated in this TR experience found their symbol to be a breakthrough. It provided a metaphor they could follow each day. Some hung their symbols in prominent places as a reminder, others later turned them into personal jewelry to wear daily.

Teachers . . . This ritual can be used and modified with language appropriate for use at any level, from elementary to graduate school, with remarkable outcomes. The Life Symbol Ritual is ideal for younger children and adults with limited or no reading skills. (We recommend that children use extra long pipe cleaners.) A writing project or journal entry could follow the sharing.

4
Appreciation Celebration

Almost daily, it seems, we are bombarded with negativity. The news is full of death and destruction. We swallow criticism from bosses, spouses or ourselves. Sometimes it is hard to maintain a positive outlook when you don't feel that your actions are appreciated. This ritual, the Appreciation Celebration, provides a time for loving, blessing and appreciating ourselves and each other.

YOU'LL NEED

Paper; pen or pencil; and a tape recorder with a blank tape for each person present (optional).

THE RITUAL

Have people sit in a circle. Ask for one person at a time to come into the center. They can sit or stand, with their eyes open or closed — whatever makes them comfortable. Ask people to tell them something positive: a blessing, praise, appreciation or even just a positive word. The person receiving the positive words should say nothing and really take in what is being said to her. Each person takes a turn in the center. The people in the circle doing the blessing are not to be called on or required to speak in order. Anyone can talk, but no one has to talk. Encourage people to make the comments as individualized as possible.

People should be warned against making negative remarks or qualified comments such as, "You have made a lot of progress, but you still need to overcome your fear." The comments or blessings should be *totally* positive and supportive.

Designate one person in the group as the recording secretary and have him write down as many of the statements of appreciation as possible. Give it to the person receiving appreciation as a personal record of what was shared. It is also nice if a tape recorder is used to make a personal tape for each person, which they can keep as personal mementos of the experience. If your organization is on a tight budget, each person can supply her own tape, or tapes can be made available for purchase.

In addition to the verbal celebration, a non-verbal component can be added. After everyone has taken his turn, go through the same procedure, but have one or more people come up to the person standing in the middle and express their love and positive regard nonverbally. For instance, one person may want to take the person's hand and clasp it firmly — indicating strong friendship. Another person may want to give a good pat on the back — indicating encouragement. Others may want to take the person for a brief walk, dance, hug or pick up the person.

This last experience is voluntary. If a person does not want to go into the center, he should not be required to do so.

The Appreciation Celebration is effective as a closing to a group experience. We often include the celebration as a closing for all of our retreats. It allows people the opportunity to share with one another what they have received during their time together and often some significant, life-transforming insights are offered.

WHO CAN USE THE RITUAL

Families . . . This is an effective way for families to show love and appreciation for each other. Regular Appreciation Celebrations encourage both children and parents. We all need positive strokes from time to time.

Therapists . . . The Appreciation Celebration can be particularly useful in helping people accept compliments. It also encourages self-esteem and self-awareness.

Spiritual Leaders . . . Performed in retreat settings, classes, and other small group settings, this TR can be an effective tool for young people after they have been together for some time and have a good knowledge of each other's lives. It is a marvelous celebration of faith and spiritual growth at any time, for any age group.

Recovery Groups . . . Good used in small groups as a way to affirm and acknowledge one's sobriety, progress and sobriety anniversaries. Can also build group support and appreciation for sponsors and other helpers.

TRANSFORMATION STORY

The Appreciation Celebration was used as a closing to one of our organization's young adults' retreats. Ken, a young, handsome golf pro with an outgoing personality, was a participant in the week-long activities. Although Ken appeared to have everything going for him, he had a problem that gave him much pain: a speech impediment that caused him to stutter when he spoke. It often took Ken a long time to share his thoughtful insights because of his stammering and stuttering.

As the retreat ended, Ken's group stood together and "bombarded" each other with positive thoughts of love, support and appreciation for each other. Ken received many thoughts of appreciation, love and support. He was so moved by their words of praise that he began to thank everyone. As Ken spoke, the group members looked at each other in astonishment. Ken was not stuttering! He continued talking for a few more minutes, and one amazed young woman in the group said, "Ken! Do you notice anything different? You're not stuttering anymore!"

Before the eyes of each person, a miracle occurred — a miracle of love and appreciation. The group asked many questions: "How could this happen? What happened to change a lifetime pattern of stuttering?"

Perhaps we can never scientifically explain how Ken overcame his impediment, but we can appreciate what did happen. Two years later Ken returned for another retreat, and he continued to speak with ease and confidence, all because of the love and appreciation from a small group of caring people.

5
Letter To God, Higher Power Or The Quest

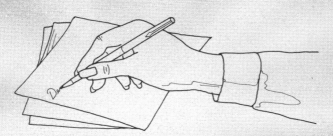

In the hustle and bustle of everyday life, it is easy to lose contact with our spiritual nature. We can get so caught up in the mechanics of living that we forget that we are a part of a much larger whole. This ritual — which is called the Letter to God, Higher Power or the Quest, depending on your orientation — can help to consciously connect, in a very personal way, to Spirit or a power greater than oneself.

YOU'LL NEED

Writing paper; pen or pencil; and an envelope.

THE RITUAL

The Letter to God can follow the Burning Bowl Ceremony described in Chapter One, or any other ritual in which something has been released. It is important to remember that when something is released in our lives we need to replace it with something better. The Letter to God can help us seek a new direction, by tapping into our spirit — our inner power from which we can always find the answers to our questions and the strength to carry out our plans.

Following the Burning Bowl ritual, people return to their seats and write their Letter to God. This is a very personal and individual experience. No one sees the letter but the writer. The TR facilitator may give suggestions such as, "What does your greatest and deepest wisdom want to communicate to you? What wants to be realized and lived out as your life? What understanding or healing is seeking to come to you at this moment? What new strength, peace and plenty is even now knocking at the door of your consciousness, asking to be part of you?"

After the letter is complete, each person seals their envelope and writes their address on it. The letters are collected and stored in a secure place for about five months. At that time, they are mailed back to their authors. By reading the letter again months later, people can reinforce what they have put out to the universe. The re-reading is an affirmation of the promises made to oneself and God.

The Letter to God can also be used as a closing ritual to any other TR experience, at the end of a workshop or a retreat.

LETTER *FROM* GOD

A letter *from* God is another effective process for establishing an inner dialogue. The Letter from God can be prayer in its truest sense, allowing us to open ourselves to a deeper contact with our Divine Self.

Eric Butterworth gives us helpful guidance in the process of our writing our Letter from God when he counsels:

> So prayer is not something we do *to* God, or a ceremony we perform *for* God. It is an experience of our own God-potential . . . We do not really pray *to* God, rather we pray *from* a consciousness of God. Prayer is not conditioning God with our needs, but conditioning our lives with the activity of God. Prayer is self-realization, self-expansion. It is getting recentered within, and re-establishing ourselves in the flow of the infinite creative process.

Ask people to write as if God, Higher Power, The Quest or Divine Potential were actually speaking to them. True communion with God is greater than addressing petitions *to* God, rather communicating *from* the consciousness of God within us.

Since this turning within and letting our intuition or inner voice of wisdom speak or write through us may seem quite different, here is an example of what it might be like. Remember, we are writing from the perspective that the Higher Power is a supportive and loving presence.

A LETTER FROM GOD TO DAVID

Dear David,

Thank you for the opportunity to share some important ideas with you. Thank you for turning within to listen. All I want for you is to live fully — a healthy, happy life, with consideration for yourself, others and the world.

David, please do be receptive to the beauty and people around you. Play more and let yourself smile. Lighten up on yourself and others. Be conscious of your good points (as I am) and don't be so hard on others. Please make sure you exercise regularly and eat healthy food. I don't mean to sound "paternal," because I am really your inner wisdom guiding you to take care of your self and your body temple.

Stay in contact with me each day, especially as you wake up and go to sleep; turn to me often and let me commune with you. Remember, you are wonderful. I love you and am always with you and for you. You are never alone.

Love,

Your Higher Power

As you did with the Letter to God, seal your Letter from God in an envelope and mail it back at a designated time.

WHO CAN USE THE RITUAL

Individuals . . . The Letter to God can be an ongoing spiritual experience for anyone. Simply write your letter and give it to a trusted friend. Tell them that when they feel it is the right time, they can mail the letter back to you.

Families . . . Families can join together and write their letters on a holiday or other special occasion and put them away for a designated period of time. The Letter to God can help bond families spiritually. Children can learn from an early age how to get in touch with their spirit and inner strength.

Therapists . . . Can help clients open themselves to the idea of mind, body and spirit working together to provide guidance from an inner resource. The Letter to God can begin the process of dialogue with an aspect of themselves they may not normally come in contact with. This letter may be shared as part of the therapy session. In group counseling, the Letter to God can be a catalyst for group interaction. It can also be a private experience, as described earlier.

Spiritual Leaders . . . The Letter to God combined with the Burning Bowl Ritual can be a powerful experience for a church community. The rituals can be used as part of a New Year's Eve or Lenten celebration.

Recovery Groups . . . To work as part of a 12-Step program, we suggest calling the ritual: Letter to Higher Power. Groups can begin by first defining Higher Power. A variety of views will likely be presented and a discussion of the difference between spirituality and religious beliefs can also take place. The letter can follow the Burning Bowl Ritual or it can be an independent experience. Letters can be shared or private. In either case, mail each of the letters back after a designated period of time.

Teachers . . . A different use for this TR in the classroom is for teachers to have students view their lives as a quest for something meaningful. Discussion can take place about what it means to be on a quest. The teacher can use "the quest" song from "The Man of La Mancha" whose lyrics invoke us, "To dream the impossible dream." Stories of life quests can be read, then each student can write a Letter to the Quest. This letter can be shared or kept private, then filed and returned to the student at a designated time, perhaps at the end of the term or year.

6
White Stone Ritual

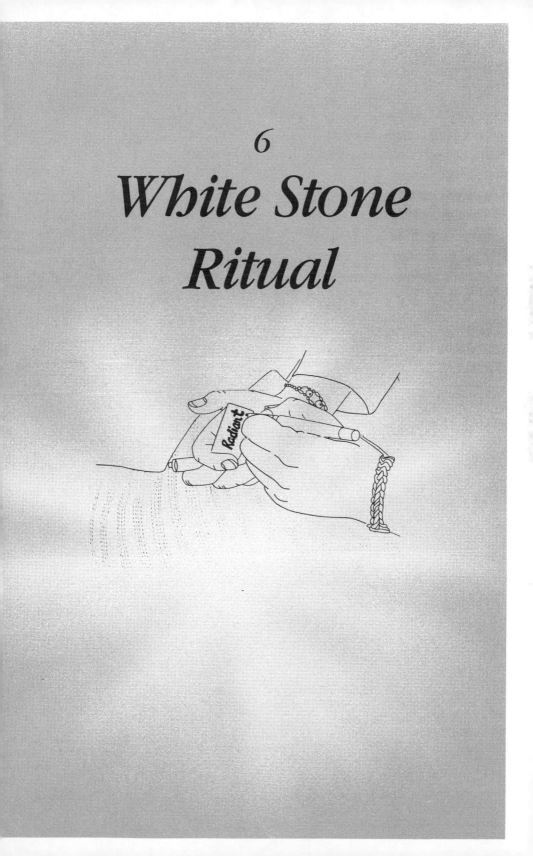

Our identities are shaped by many things. Names are our labels and play a large part in defining who we are, yet they are chosen for us. The White Stone Ritual gives us the opportunity to choose a new spiritual name for ourselves, a name that resonates with qualities we wish to develop. It is a way to mark a new beginning in life or the optimistic start to a new year.

YOU'LL NEED

A small slab of white tile or marble, approximately a one inch by two inch square (can be ordered from a local tile and marble company and cut to size); and a pencil.

THE RITUAL

Give each person a white stone and a pencil. Begin by leading them in a meditation or time of inner reflection like this:

The inspiration for the White Stone Ritual comes from the Bible passage in *Revelation 2:17*:

"They that hath an ear, let them hear what the Spirit saith unto the churches; to they that overcometh will I give to eat of the hidden manna, and will give them a white stone, and in the stone a *new name* written, which no person knoweth saving they that receiveth it."

Adapted from King James version.

To those that overcame, who moved forward with faith, a new name was given. Today, we will meditate on our new name, for each of us here has overcome adversity. We have freed ourselves to live more fully, conscious of the activity of Spirit in every aspect of our lives and the creative life force. In this recognition, we free ourselves to live more fully, releasing ourselves from bondage, the prison of limiting thoughts about ourselves, each other and our world.

The custom in the ancient days, when a prisoner was released from prison or bondage, was to give him or her a white stone to take with them to show that they were free. Only people who were freed would be given the white stone. Symbolically the stone that you hold in your hand now represents your freedom. Feel the smooth stone with your hand, and know that it represents release from old ways of thinking — the limiting ways of expressing your creative life force and spirit.

Say to yourself, "I am free, I have a clean slate, I can choose any moment to begin again. This is a new beginning, a new day, a new opportunity."

Begin to reflect on a new name. Let it come to you easily, without trying to make it happen. Let a name come to you that marks your new beginning. Feel the stone in your hand. Hear it beckon to you. Spirit has decreed a name for you to be written on the stone. What will your life be called? Is it a name? Is it a title? Is it a quality? A new state of being? Start with the words, "I am," then express what you want to see happen in your life. What will be written on your stone? (Period of silence.)

A thankfulness flows over us as we receive our new name. Along with it comes the power and guidance to achieve all that we desire. This is our new name. We see it. We decree it. We are on the path to gaining greater insight and awareness and mark a new beginning.

If it is appropriate to the setting, group sharing might follow the time of reflection and writing to build bridges between one's inner world and relationships with family, friends and spiritual community. In a church setting with many people, sharing can take place during the fellowship time following the service.

The children and youth classes can also participate in this special ritual with assistance from their teachers. Because of the highly personal nature of each revelation, the utmost respect needs to be shown for each person's sharing.

WHO CAN USE THE RITUAL

Individuals . . . Individuals can release self-deprecating thoughts and begin to see themselves in a new light. This is a creative exercise in connecting with life guidance.

Therapists . . . Individuals, couples and small groups can use this TR to rename one's life, mark a new beginning and deepen relationships with others.

Spiritual Leaders . . . Can use the TR as a rite of passage into the new year by inviting congregants to release the limitations and mistakes of the past. By taking a new spiritual name, congregants can use their spiritual power to give their lives more meaning. For example, Yom Kippur represents the experience of regeneration and going forth into new live expression. Looking at the inner process of each person, rather than a ceremony intended to gain God's favor, Yom Kippur can be a time of letting go of the limitations and mistakes of the past, reflecting on who we are, and looking for ways to a better life, family, community and world. Atonement is, we feel, a knowing of at-one-ment with the Source of Life; the names of seekers written in the Book of Life mean, to us, a reminder to be fully alive, and a blessing to ourselves, our families, neighbors and world community. Renewed within, we go forward into a year that will be new and better.

Recovery Programs . . . Adopting a new name can help those in recovery release compulsive habits and behaviors that are holding them captive. They can let go of the limited view of recovery "from" something and, through their own self-definition, see a more expansive view of one's life as recovery "to" something better.

7
World Celebration Ceremony

The world is a beautiful patchwork quilt of diverse cultures held together by the common threads of belief and humanity. Yet sometimes the differences that make our world so interesting are causes for strife and social unrest. The World Celebration Ceremony is a symbolic means of honoring and celebrating the diversity of cultures and beliefs, so that we can work toward living together in peace.

YOU'LL NEED

Seven candles and candle holders.

THE RITUAL

Gather together as a family or group of people to celebrate diversity and the oneness of humanity. Readings and candle lighting can be done by designating participants before the ceremony.

Opening

May the leaders of all countries and the people of all races be guided to understand that we are all physically and spiritually one: physically one because we are descendants of common parents, the primordial father and mother; spiritually one because we are the immortal children of one Spirit, eternally linked in the family of humanity.

First reading and candle lighting

O Cosmic Light, in this silence take away the darkness of age. May we realize that thy light illumines all paths. We honor those who walk the path of Hinduism. (Light the first candle.)

We, too, feel the great Om of Spirit as it invites us to cultivate peace in our minds, in our hearts, in our world. (Observe silence.)

Second reading and candle lighting

Blessed by the power of Spirit's illumination, we understand the Truth of those who follow the teachings of Buddha in their quest for peace: "There is no greater happiness than peace." We honor brothers and sisters who follow the path of Buddha. (Light the second candle.)

In thy blessed light I shall remain awake forever. (Observe silence.)

Third reading and candle lighting

The Cosmic Light illumines the minds and hearts of those who follow the Tao. There is a thing inherent and natural which existed before heaven and earth. It stands alone and never changes. It pervades everywhere and never becomes exhausted. I do not know its name. I call it Tao and name it Supreme. Its nature is peace, its essence is light.

We honor those who follow the Tao. (Light the third candle.)

The Tao follows its intrinsic nature, peace and light. (Observe silence.)

Fourth reading and candle lighting

I am beholding the Light through the eyes of all. I am working through the hands of all. I am walking through all feet. The followers of the prophet, Mohammed, in their awareness of the Great Allah and from the Book, The Koran, echo these words: "I will guide you from the darkness of war to the light of peace."

We honor those who walk the path of Mohammed. (Light the fourth candle.)

"And Allah calleth you into the abode of peace . . . and guideth ye in the straight way." (Observe silence.)

Fifth reading and candle lighting

Again the Light of Spirit manifests as wisdom behind human reasoning. We see the deeper significance of the Judaic covenant from Isaiah: "And my people shall dwell in a peaceable habitation . . . and in quiet resting places."

We honor those who walk the path of Judaism.
(Light the fifth candle.)

We make this scripture true as we transform fear, resentment and greed into love, understanding and sharing in God's Holy Light.
(Observe silence.)

Sixth reading and candle lighting

I will follow the shepherd of peace, guided by the star of wisdom to the birth of Christ consciousness; the Light of love illuminates all who walk the path of Christianity. I honor those who walk the path of Jesus.
(Light the sixth candle.)

"Blessed are the peacemakers for they shall be called the children of God."
(Observe silence.)

Seventh reading and candle lighting

"Come sit with me and let us smoke the pipe of peace in understanding. Let us touch. Let us, each to the other, be a Gift as is the buffalo. Let us be meat to nourish each other that we all may grow."

Our Native American brothers and sisters called it the Sun Dance. They explained it this way:

"This mound of earth is the sacred mountain. These four stakes around the mound are your first four chiefs: one is North, one is South, one is East, one is West. This fifth stick in the center of the mound is the Peace Chief. This chief is the one all the rest dance to . . ."

We honor those who follow the spirit of the Peace Chief. (Light the seventh candle.)

Our own vision quest is the peace, peace, peace. (Observe silence.)

Conclusion

I am the All, from which All proceedeth. With thy mind and understanding fixed firmly upon me, Thou shall come to me. By whatever path you seek me, you will find me. We respect and recognize our sisters and brothers who walk the non-sectarian path, who view the Absolute from a non-parochial perspective. True spirit lies beyond the realm of the visible. In each there is a spark able to kindle new fires of peace and human progress. When enough fires are burning, they will create a new dawn of spiritual understanding. The flame of a great peace will be formed. Humankind will advance to a higher level of civilization.

Responsive affirmation

(Read then repeat together:)

I am a spark of the Infinite.

I am the darkness and the Light.

The God of peace directs my thoughts and my actions.

The ceremony could be concluded with a circle dance, a song such as "Let There Be Peace On Earth," by Sy Miller and Jill Jackson or "It's In Everyone Of Us," by David Pomerantz — or simply dismiss in silence.

WHO CAN USE THE RITUAL

Families . . . A great way to teach cultural diversity and respect for different belief systems.

Spiritual Leaders . . . Can incorporate the ritual into the weekly Sunday worship as a special service, or as an independent ceremony held on a specific occasion such as World Peace Day.

8
Love Picture Ritual

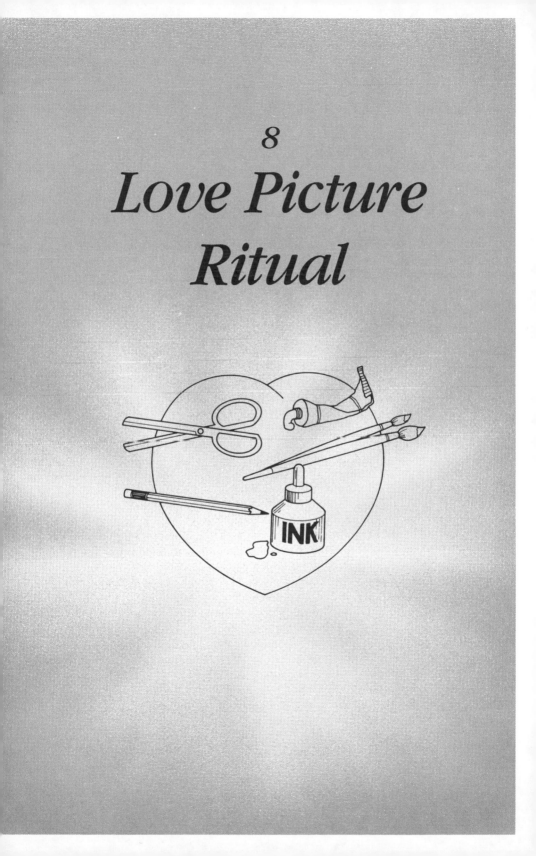

People often have a difficult time expressing their feelings verbally. This can be especially true in group situations. The Love Picture Ritual is a way to open the barriers to communication through artistic expression on paper. It is a group experience emphasizing accepting and giving group support and love.

YOU'LL NEED

A roll of butcher block paper that can be cut into large pieces, or a roll of white paper; crayons; colored construction paper; colored chalk; scissors; paint; old magazines that can be cut up; glue; tape; glitter; leaves that have fallen from the trees; pieces of cloth; aluminum foil; and any available art supplies.

THE RITUAL

The Love Picture Ritual is a group process with a focus on learning about our feelings, both individually and as a part of the group. We want to express artistically on paper who we are and how we feel about each other. The paper is rolled out on the floor or table. People can draw, write messages or questions or cut and paste using the magazines and art supplies.

To get people thinking, questions can be posed to the group such as: "How do I feel about myself in this group? How do I feel about others in the group? How can I best use the support of others as I grow and change? What does it feel like for me to ask for help? How would you describe the experiences of love, support or help?"

Continue by telling the group: "We will communicate by drawing or writing on the paper. It is a fun way to better understand ourselves and each other. You can write or draw whatever you want. Put something on the paper which describes your feelings about yourself and also where you are at in the group. Be original. As you see others write or draw things, you may write or draw in response as a way to communicate with them. For instance, someone may draw a wall, you think, to represent themselves. You might draw a rose climbing up the wall as your message or feeling about them to indicate that they are overcoming the wall.

The Love Picture Ritual should be completed in silence so that all the group's energy will go toward expressing their feelings on the paper. Nonverbal communication is okay — such as a smile, nod, shake of the head or pointing.

When you feel that people have pretty much finished what they are doing, have them gather around the picture so all can see. Ask people to share what they felt the others in the group meant by some of their original designs, symbols or expressions. Individuals can share the meanings of their drawings. Questions could be asked such as, "How did you feel when Jane drew that rose climbing up your wall?"

Remind people to talk about themselves in the first person. When they are sharing, have them talk to each other directly. That is, if someone says, "I think a lot of Jane. She seems like she is looking for a greater sense of freedom to be herself." Tell the speaker, "Please tell Jane that." In other words, do not let people talk *about* others, have them talk *with* others. It is much more healing and powerful.

To close, stand in a circle around the group portrait, with arms around each other's shoulders, and have people speak a word of appreciation or tell of the insight they gained from the TR experience.

WHO CAN USE THE RITUAL

Families . . . A delightful experience in which members can create a visual image of their role in the family, and come to an understanding about how the family works as a system. This experience can be shared by just the immediate family or the extended family, perhaps as part of a reunion celebration. Questions can be asked such as: "How do I feel about myself in this family? How do I feel about others in the family? What is it like for me to be loved and supported by the family? How could we best support each other? What does it feel like to ask for help in our family?"

Therapists . . . This TR is a great group process for understanding individual members and their relationship to the group. You could operate around a theme, such as the experience of group support in growth and change.

Spiritual Leaders . . . A retreat is a good setting for this ritual. A reading of the Bible passage *I Corinthians 13* is a good way to open the Love Picture Ritual:

> Love is patient; love is kind; love is not envious or boastful or arrogant or rude. It does not insist on its own way; it is not irritable or resentful; it does not rejoice in wrongdoing, but rejoices in the truth. It bears all things, believes all things, hopes all things, endures all things.
>
> *I Corinthians 13, Verses 4-7*

Recovery Groups . . . A simple phrase we often use is, "I alone do it, but I never do it alone." Using this concept, build on the power of support groups for illustrating the Love Picture. Ask group members to depict the power of group support in self-discovery. The ceremony is an excellent way to help establish bonds of mutual assistance.

9
Divorce
Ceremony

Statistics show that nearly half of all marriages in the U.S. end in divorce. The process often engages couples in pitched legal battles and leaves them feeling alienated and bitter. The transition from a married state to a single one is a difficult process for all involved — adults and children alike. While the union of two people is conducted with great pomp and circumstance, the undoing of the matrimonial bond is achieved with no fanfare at all. The Divorce Ceremony was created to mark this rite of passage and help all involved begin a new life.

YOU'LL NEED

Music appropriate for a new beginning; Burning Bowl Ritual materials, including pen or pencil, paper and a wok; wedding rings.

THE RITUAL

We offer two samples of possible ceremonies done with the couple or family present:

Divorce Ceremony I

_____ and _____, we have come here today to share in a cooperative act of dissolution of the union of two people who have decided to walk separate paths. It is right and fitting that we begin this time with a word of prayer.

God, we acknowledge Your presence here with us today as these two beloved people begin new life experiences independent of one another. May each of them always know that you are with them as their source of strength to meet each new challenge, of light to walk new paths and of love to fill their hearts anew. Your strength, light and love shall never fail them now or in days to come. And so it is. Amen.

We participate in many ceremonies throughout our lives. Some are joyful and happy, some are filled with awe and wonder, while others may be filled with sadness and grief. Yet, all are rites of passage — transitions from one state of being to another. Today, we are participating in a rite of passage from a state of union to a state of separation. We endeavor to make that passage as gentle as possible without denying the pain that each of you may be feeling.

You have taken legal steps to divide into independent persons. You are now ready to walk paths that can pave the way to a new, free-standing relationship that can have very special qualities of respect and communication.

Each of you is ready to find a new sense of purpose that is truly your own. But in order that you may do this successfully, it is necessary to begin the process of releasing the past — the old hurts, fears, frustrations — and negative thoughts and emotions that might block your way. You have each given this some thought and written these barriers to happiness on sheets of paper so that they may be symbolically released in the cleansing fire.

We have the ability to restore peace and harmony to our lives. When we forgive ourselves and each other, we gain new freedom through the release of hurt and resentment that could hinder our well-being. Through forgiveness we learn and progress. You keep the memories of what was good and the wisdom of lessons learned together. You also acknowledge the pain and struggle. As you set the paper on fire, you change it from one to another. It is symbolic of the transformation of your lives from a couple to two individuals. Go forth from this moment to express greater wisdom, love and understanding.

_____ and _____, please light your paper and say, "In the Spirit of truth I am free and you are free."

Having acknowledged your freedom you are now ready to forge new identities that are yours alone. As you let go of the protective supports you found in one another, you may run into resistance from within yourselves. You may find a fear of standing alone — yet know at the depths of your being, you are never alone. God is with you — a present help — now and always.

Let Spirit's strength support you as you grieve for that which is passing away. Let your inner wisdom reveal new power to take responsibility for your lives so that you may reach your full potential. Let love renew within you a blossoming of the sense of your sacred selfhood.

Let your feelings be. Let the changes happen. Let yourselves live and love. And let the peace of Spirit fill your minds and hearts now and always. And so it is!

Divorce Ceremony II

Choose a musical selection or two that represent what the people involved are experiencing and would like to share with others.

The leader reads:

True marriage is more than the joining of two persons in the bonds of matrimony. It is a process of uniting two souls attuned to each other. True marriage is a path which kindred souls choose to walk and share together. In the course of this relationship, _____ and _____ have developed and shared love, trust and true intimacy with each other. Their souls have connected in a sacred bond. Their hearts and minds have become entwined and rooted in one another. When a separation takes place, these deep roots are pulled apart, often causing deep pain. This pain is often accompanied by questions that have no answers, and by feelings of guilt, doubt and fear. These feelings are real. These feelings don't need explanation; they need to be validated by providing comfort, support and, above all, love.

And so we gather here to lovingly support _____, _____ and their (son/daughter/children). Divorce is neither a right nor a wrong decision. It is a choice. We are given not only the ability to choose, but truly the responsibility to choose the path that will lead to our highest spiritual good and the full expression of our potential. We don't often choose a path that is free of pain, and we don't always remain on the path we once chose. As our spiritual unfolding continues, we know that we are doing our best. We will make mistakes, but that only means we are choosing life and are willing to risk.

In the sixth chapter of Luke, Jesus taught us, "Judge not, and you will not be judged; condemn not, and you will not be condemned; forgive, and you will be forgiven." (Luke 6:37)

And so today we affirm our forgiveness. We let go of the past. We seek to release fear, doubt and guilt and fill the spaces left between us with compassion. We wish each other well and desire only good for all concerned.

Although this ceremony commemorates the day of your divorce, your relationship does not end. There can never completely be a separation between you. For always there will be a past that is shared. And always there will be concerns of the present. Certain bonds remain between you. Let these ties call forth your wisdom and goodness; let them be ties that strengthen and support.

Leader: Please repeat after me:
            I, _____ (husband's name)
Husband: I, _____
Leader: I, _____ (wife's name)
Wife: I, _____
Leader: Hereby affirm my place in the ending of our marriage.
Couple: Hereby affirm my place in the ending of our marriage.

Leader: Now I enter into a new relationship with you.
Couple: Now I enter into a new relationship with you.
Leader: I treasure the beautiful things we have shared.
Couple: I treasure the beautiful things we have shared.
Leader: I desire only good for you (and our children).
Couple: I desire only good for you (and our children).
Leader: Above all, I promise to respect you as an individual.
Couple: Above all, I promise to respect you as an individual.
Leader: This is my pledge.
Couple: This is my pledge.

Leader: (To wife.) May I have your ring?
            Let us pray, let the return of this ring be the release from a pledge once undertaken and now outlived. As what you exchanged is now returned, so shall you be free to enter into a new life, a new marriage and a new love. May you separate now, not with regret for love unachieved, but with hope and belief in love yet possible. Amen.
            (Repeat for husband, if double ring-ceremony.)
Leader: (Returns ring to husband.) And so, as you, ___ and _____, have stated to one another your intention to live apart and to create lives independent; as you have further declared your common commitment to the well-being of one another and to all whose lives you touch; a commitment to respect yourself and each other, I now pronounce your marriage dissolved. I summon society — family, friends and strangers — to honor the decision you have made and the separate paths you have chosen.
Leader: (Asks child/children to come forward and stand between the parents.) This separation is in no

way your responsibility; it is only that of your
parents. Your presence in their lives remains
most important. You brought joy to their marriage when you were born and you continue to
bring them joy.

Husband: (To child or each child.)_____, I am and always
will be grateful for you. Nothing can ever erase
my love for you, even though your mother
and I have chosen to live apart. I give you this
ring as a symbol of eternal love. It has no beginning and no ending. Such is my love for
you. (kiss)

Wife: (To child or each child.)_____, I am and always
will be grateful for you. Nothing can ever erase
my love for you, even though your father and
I have chosen to live apart. I give you this gold
chain as a symbol of the bond of love we share.
Each link is a symbol of a happy and beautiful
moment we have had together. (kiss)
(Parents put chain through ring and fasten
around child's neck. Repeat for each child — an
option is to give other symbolic gifts or just
have a gold chain for each child without the
ring exchange.)

Leader: Let us pray. May all that is noble, lovely and
true, all that is enriching and creative and all
that is beautiful, be in your lives and abide in
your homes, forever. Amen.
This concludes our service.

WHO CAN USE THE RITUAL

Individuals . . . Sometimes it is not possible for a couple to
move through this experience together, but the need to honor the
transition still exists. We suggest that men and women create
their own rite of passage as a means to put closure to the relationship. One person had the gold in their wedding ring melted

down and restyled into a symbol that was significant of the new beginning. The old was incorporated into the new to symbolize moving forward with life.

Families . . . Families can join together in this time to grieve the loss and look toward the future by creating an atmosphere of mutual support beyond the marriage. This is vitally needed for the children who often feel at fault. The ceremony can help them internalize the change and be reassured of their parents' ongoing love and support.

Therapists . . . The process of planning and participating in a Divorce Ceremony can help families and couples bring closure to marriage and move on with their lives.

Spiritual Leaders . . . If the couple was joined in a religious ceremony, in the presence of clergy, it can be healing to have clergy take an active role in the changing family relationship. Many families fall away from their spiritual community at the time of divorce, and the support and love of the clergy can be effective in communicating the message that the family is still wanted as part of the church community.

TRANSFORMATION STORY (FROM GAY)

A woman who had been coming to me for counseling phoned me one day with a problem: she had just ended her marriage through a painful divorce but didn't feel closure, for many reasons, including the fact that she didn't even have to appear in court. The partnership was legally dissolved, and for all intents and purposes she could move on with her life, but because she was still emotionally attached, she was stuck in a sort of mental purgatory. She was coming to me, she said, to design a ritual that would help her end the marriage in her mind's eye and move into a better space.

We discussed some of her ideas. She suggested doing some writing about the relationship, reflecting on the growth, the pain, the healing and forgiveness of the past. She added that she would like to read her work out loud to me and then burn it along with some of the pictures of the two of them together. I suggested taking the ashes, burying them and then planting a small tree on top of them. That way, as she looks out in her yard, she will be reminded of how she is branching out in life. This simple ceremony became a rite of passage of her own creation.

10
Home Blessing And Cleansing Ritual

When we first move into a house, it is merely a building without any imprint from our lives. The Home Blessing and Cleansing Ritual is a way to bless and ready the home for the new life that is brought into it. Blessing the rooms of a house that we've occupied for some time protects us spiritually and gives the sense of symbolically "cleansing" the abode and reinforcing the good times that we want to experience there.

A special blessing for each room of the home is provided.

YOU'LL NEED

A "home blessing decal" for the windows of your home (see appendix for where to purchase this item); you may also include a favorite incense — sage is particularly nice — which is good for cleansing.

THE RITUAL

Go into each room of your home and use some of the following blessings. Feel free to create your own blessings and have other members of the family participate. As the blessings are being spoken, a small amount of incense can be burned in each room.

Of course, the content and approach to consecrating a living space can be adapted to make the ceremony appropriate to one's lifestyle or circumstances.

Kitchen

We bless and consecrate this room to the preparation of nourishment. All the food prepared here is blessed so that it will carry nourishment for the soul as well as the body. May the tasks done in this room be accomplished as a labor of love. May this place represent a workshop of love where the bounty of God's provision is made pleasant to the taste.

Dining Room

We bless and consecrate this room to the partaking of nourishment and the fellowship of all who join around this table. May the meals here be enjoyed in a relaxed atmosphere and seasoned with good fellowship and cheerfulness. May we come from this place each mealtime strengthened both in body and soul.

Living Room

We bless and consecrate this room to the art of living — to expanding the consciousness of abundant life. The living room is the altar of the home, for here the family gathers to share its love. This room is the matrix of love for the home — and love is the essence of life.

This is a room of *tenderness*, where each person feels free to say, "I love you," to the other members of the family and friends. It is a place where *appreciation* finds expression.

This is a room of *courtesy*. Impatience and complaint are removed from this place and understanding prevails.

This is a room of *sociability*, where wholesome and pleasant entertainment are enjoyed.

This is a room where *understanding* of each other's temperament is a hallmark. It is a place of self-control.

This is a room where *honesty*, *truthfulness* and *straightforwardness* are evidenced. It is a place of trust.

This is a *living* room, where life is enjoyed and understood.

Bedrooms

We bless and consecrate these rooms to rest and refreshment. In the quiet of the night hours, this is a place for the regathering of strength for the coming day. May the cares and burdens of the day be left outside this room. May dreams come that bring guidance and understanding.

Children's Room

May this room be a safe haven for our children and their pets and special toys. May they always feel that God is watching over them. (You might want to hang up a picture or symbol in the room to reinforce the feeling of a safe haven. In our children's room, we hung an old family heirloom, a picture of an angel watching over two children as they crossed a bridge.)

Couple's Room

In this room may each embrace the other in love and affection at the end of each day. May the bed be a source of great comfort, compassion and unconditional love.

Bathroom

We bless and consecrate the bathroom and the sharing of this vital place. May each take refuge when needed and may peace reign supreme as this space is shared with each person in the home.

Closing

May we be mindful that this place is more than wood, nails and mortar. For a house to be a home, it must have an atmosphere — a mood. We anticipate the mood of this home to be one of love and the reverence and joy of prayer. We know that each room does not need an altar of wood or stone. The spirit of prayer prevails in the hearts of those who dwell here, and each room is a living altar.

WHO CAN USE THE RITUAL

Individuals . . . A personal blessing and consecration of a living space helps the house feel more like a home in a shorter amount of time. It also helps in clearing the energy from the previous owner or occupant. This ritual can also be used to consecrate a new place of business.

Families . . . A spiritual addition to the traditional housewarming experience can add meaning to a move. Join together in a celebration dinner following the blessing.

Spiritual Leaders . . . This ritual may be chosen for the blessing of a new home or one that's been lived in for a while, for any member of the spiritual community. This can also be adapted to bless a new church building.

11
A Walk With God

AUGURIES OF INNOCENCE
To see a World in a grain of sand
And a Heaven in a wild flower,
Hold Infinity in the palm of your hand
And Eternity in an hour.

— *William Blake*

One of the most heart-wrenching side-effects of our fast-paced society is loneliness. We get in our cars alone and drive to work along with all the other faceless workers alone in their cars. We may rush to our homes without ever stopping to say hello to the next-door neighbor. Some of the loneliest people live in the most heavily populated cities. They don't feel a part of any group or community. Many people try to find a remedy for their isolation in self-damaging behavior such as drinking or drug use. While there are many reasons for the sense of isolation felt by people, perhaps one of the strongest is the lack of a connection to a Higher Power or to the wonders of nature that surround them every day. Those who are connected to a Higher Power or to Mother Nature may sometimes find themselves alone, but they are never lonely.

This ceremony gives people the experience of a greater awareness of connection to God, the earth and all living things.

YOU'LL NEED

A copy of the Walk with God script, as listed on the next page, for each person; paper; pencils; markers; crayons; tape; glue; other art supplies; and an outdoor area where you can walk.

THE RITUAL

Give everyone a script and ask them to read and follow the directions. Make sure people have comfortable walking shoes, jackets and hats as needed.

Script For A Closer Walk With God

Before you begin the activities outlined in this script, please take a moment to affirm silently: "God, I desire a closer walk with you."

The following walk is to be taken alone so one might realize that even without the company of others, there is no aloneness. Walk away from your starting point and the people who are with you. After walking about 50 yards stop and look around you. Notice what is far away and what is close to you. Look up at the sky and down at the earth you are standing on. Take note of things at an intermediate distance. What are you feeling? What impresses you most about the surroundings?

Before continuing your walk declare: "God, I am surrounded by your presence."

Slowly begin to walk in the direction that feels best for you. Feel the earth beneath your feet. What is its texture? Is it easy to walk on? What effect does the weather have on you? Is the sun warm on your skin? Does the unseen air that surrounds you make itself known to you? Breathe deeply. Sense the air passing through your lips or nostrils.

Before resuming the closer walk affirm: "God, I feel your presence."

Walk quickly for 50 feet. Pause for a moment and jog for 50 feet. Pause again and rest. When you are ready, move forward as if you are a leaf driven by the wind: turn, bend, stop, start, move your arms around you and above your head. Be the leaf and sense the strength and support of Spirit. Discover what you sense God's plan is for you.

Rest from your turning and moving, but let your mind be compelled by what you cannot see. Without breaking the flow, observe and perhaps record any thoughts or feelings that seem important.

Before continuing the closer walk with God, affirm: "The wisdom of God directs my path."

Continue your walk with God and let your powers of observation sense the many sounds around you. Listen to the sounds of your walking. Stop and close your eyes. Listen to the sounds your walking has masked. Listen to the rhythms of your own body: your breathing and your heartbeat. Walk again. What sounds can be heard above the sound of your walking? Pause again and listen for the wind or faint sounds in the distance. What sounds originate nearby and which have distant sources? Which sounds are pleasing and contribute to your peace? Are there sounds that are disturbing?

Prepare to walk again, but first speak silently these words: "God, I am open and receptive to your still, small voice."

Continue walking, but as you do, look for a secluded place where you can sit and be still for a time. Let yourself be drawn naturally to this place, and sit in silence with your senses attuned to your surroundings. Describe your outer surroundings. Do they relate to the world inside you? What are you thinking? What are you feeling? Have your feelings or thoughts changed since the beginning of your walk? If so, how?

Speak what is most natural for you now: "God, I have found you in stillness and in rest."

When you feel guided, rise and proceed leisurely at your own pace. Amble rather than walk. Become sensitive to any fragrances in the air — walk to the nearest plant and become aware of its fragrance. If it is appropriate, hold it in your hand and feel its texture.

Before continuing the journey speak these words: "God, I feel you in everything I touch."

Now begin to return to your group. Speak to no one, and as you walk, pause and touch as many things as you can. Touch the grass. Walk barefoot if you like. Is the grass warm or cool to the touch? Hug a tree on your return. Hug a person on your return. Let love empower you. God is with you — a constant companion — a part of everything and everyone.

As you continue to return to your group, notice the new vision you have of the earth and yourself. New portals have opened to you. Your heart is pure and you see God in every-thing, and everything in God.

Just before you enter the room, affirm: "God, I am the life you are."

Enter the room, and as you read these instructions, please continue to observe the silence that has now become so precious to you.

In the room you will find some paper and markers, pen-cils, pens and other art supplies. Using these materials, ex-press as best you can what this walk has meant to you or what you have discovered about yourself or some aspect of life. You may want to illustrate your experience or write a poem, letter or narrative.

Following the completion of the writing or drawing, each person may share their personal reflections and the draw-ings may be hung around the room in gallery style for others to observe at their leisure.

We have found it a very meaningful experience to some-times substitute God in the script with the concept of Mother

Earth or Mother Nature. Because of the outdoor setting, this association is in some ways more powerful.

WHO CAN USE THE RITUAL

Individuals . . . The experience can be used to enhance one's appreciation of life and all living things.

Families . . . A fun ritual for the family to join in together and celebrate God in the beauty of the earth and in each other.

Therapists . . . The walk is a group experience therapists can use to help people feel grounded and connected to something greater than themselves.

Spiritual Leaders . . . A group experience congregants can use to feel the sense of "God in us and us in God." Read this passage from Psalms 19:1-4: "The heavens are telling the glory of God; they are a marvelous display of God's craftsmanship. Day and night they keep on telling about God. Without a word or sound, silent in the skies, their message reaches out to all worlds." (From *The Living Bible.*)

Recovery Groups . . . A group ritual to provide people in recovery with a sense of a higher power that is lifegiving and sustaining. Also helps to ground the individuals and remind them that they are never alone.

Teachers . . . The concept of Mother Earth or Mother Nature can be substituted for God in the script. The creation of the poem, letter, drawing or narrative can be shared as a class project. The experience can be included as a writing project or as a springboard for discussions on preserving the earth's environment and honoring nature. A discussion on the rituals of indigenous people and how they worship the earth can also be included.

12
Empowerment Walk

ONE STEP MORE
A hill is not too hard to climb
Taken one step at a time.
One step is not too much to take;
One try is not too much to make.
One step, one try, one song, one smile
Will shortly stretch into a mile.
To reach the goal you started for,
Take one step more, take one step more!
— From *What God Is Like*
James Dillet Freeman

Along life's journey, we are often overwhelmed with difficult situations or seemingly insurmountable tasks. Sometimes our goals seem so out of reach that we just want to give up on ever realizing them. When looked at as a whole, it is easy to see why some tasks seem indomitable or goals unreachable — the whole picture can sometimes be frightening. But if you take that whole picture and apportion it, concentrating on the small pieces, then the task doesn't seem so horrible and you realize that you will eventually complete it — you will succeed. Marathon runners don't think about the whole race — that would be too overwhelming. Instead, they break the races into parts, a step at a time, until they cross the finish line.

The resources necessary to help people overcome obstacles in their lives to reach their goals are not found in bottles or even on bookshelves. All of the powers necessary to help us overcome adversity are contained within each of us. We all have the ability to live to our full potential if we tap into this resource. The Empowerment Walk provides a rite of passage experience to affirm the innate power shared within and between all people to help them on the path to living out their dreams. Groups leave feeling energized and ready to enter the world to be a power of good and service to others.

YOU'LL NEED

A large mirror on which words can be written; an easel to set the mirror at eye level; about 12 feet of heavy plastic carpet runner; a permanent black marker; and quiet, meditative background music.

THE RITUAL

Before getting into the details of this ceremony, it is best to explain its logistics. The mirror is set up at the beginning of the plastic runner. The runner should be placed on carpet or, if used on a bare surface, taped so that it doesn't slip. Using the marker, draw footprints on the runner. The footprints should be spaced naturally, one foot slightly in front of the other, as though someone were walking at a leisurely pace. Next to each footprint write words that represent powers. Powers that we have chosen as examples are adapted from Charles Fillmore's concept of the 12 powers of each person. They are the innate spiritual powers found in everyone and include: enthusiasm, imagination, power, judgment, understanding, love, freedom, faith, order, wisdom, strength and life. Use any words that have meaning for your group or the special feeling you would like to create with the ritual. These words may also be written on the mirror if desired.

Participants will form a tunnel at the end of the runner. With this in mind, be sure to allow plenty of room for the tunnel to be formed.

Begin by giving the entire group the instructions, and have them reflect for a few moments on each of the powers they are going to be walking with in the Empowerment Walk.

Next ask six to 10 people to form the beginning of the tunnel at the end of the runner. This way, the first people to finish walking the runner have people in the tunnel to bless them with their love and affirmations of power. After everyone has gone through the line, these beginning tunnel people can go through the entire process themselves.

Have one person at a time stand in front of the mirror and reflect on their own image, being mindful that they are a powerful part of creation. Have them look into their own eyes and look for the divine image within. Then instruct them to walk the runner slowly, placing one foot at a time on each of the marked footprints, and to observe the power that is written next to that footprint. Suggest that they feel themselves stepping into the power of love or life or whatever power is written next to the print. As much as possible, have them visualize being filled with this power, enlarged and expanded with their force. At the end of the runner have them close their eyes and prepare to go through the tunnel. As they walk slowly with eyes closed and hands open and extended, have them receive the power and affirmation as it is shared by all those participating in the Empowerment Walk.

At the end of the walk they become a part of the tunnel and bless and share their power with those who follow.

Close with a song, a reading or prayer, holding hands and feeling the power that has been shared by the group.

TRANSFORMATION STORY

Each year, a large gathering of people from our Unity community come together for a family retreat. One year, the theme was "Life Is A Dance." We were asked to do the opening day ceremony. In Unity, we teach that each person is endowed with 12 spiritual powers. These powers, as we employ them, are enthusiasm, imagination, power, judgment,

understanding, love, freedom, faith, order, wisdom, strength
and life. We choose the ways we use these powers. An excessive use of any one power can create an imbalance in our
lives and cause a great deal of stress and discomfort for
ourselves and those around us. The key is to use our 12
spiritual powers in balance and harmony.

The ceremony began with music and vocalists leading the
group in song. Music was played softly throughout the ceremony. We designed the long plastic runner with footprints
drawn on it, similar to what you might see at a dance school.
The idea we wanted to get across was that we were learning
to walk and dance through life empowered. We all are practicing the steps — walking the walk.

The experience was one of the highlights of the retreat.
Having felt the richness of the support and shared power,
many people wanted to repeat the ceremony. Many people
cried during the ritual because they had never experienced
such validation and acceptance. Some people reported spontaneous relief from various aches and pains. Many spoke of
the feeling of oneness of all life and of being intimately
connected to all people. The transformation of separateness
into oneness was a great gift we all took with us.

Life is a dance. We are all connected when we forget for
a moment the boundaries of our bodies and minds and just
become one. What a unique opportunity we shared in lifting
the veil and seeing ourselves as one beautiful, cosmic expression in motion.

WHO CAN USE THE RITUAL

Therapists . . . As a group process, this ritual is an affirmation of personal and collective power. It illustrates the
idea of taking empowering steps on the journey that is life.
Also, the ritual demonstrates the value of sharing power to
enhance group and life experiences.

Spiritual Leaders . . . Showing parishioners how to walk the path of life creatively by using and sharing our God-given powers is a great way to celebrate a Sunday service. A preliminary message from the Minister or facilitator could set up the experience with detail given to how we are stewards of our power. This is also a powerful retreat experience.

The Empowerment Walk is also used as a way to confirm and bring in new members to a spiritual community or organization. As an added feature, a scarf of a particular color for each of the spiritual powers can be placed around each person's neck as they slowly walk down the twelve-power runway while an affirmation of that power is spoken to them by people on each side of the runway.

Recovery Groups . . . This TR is an especially powerful way to use the 12 powers as the 12 steps in recovery. Emphasize the awareness that each step must be taken. Tell the group: "When we take these steps in our recovery process, we are never alone. There are many people who have walked this walk before us and we have their power and support as well as all those gathered now. To 'walk the walk' is the most important step in recovery." The Empowerment Walk is also good as an anniversary ceremony. Suggested words to use for each step are as follows:

Step 1: *Admit*	Step 7: *Humble*
Step 2: *Believe*	Step 8: *Willing*
Step 3: *Decision*	Step 9: *Amendments*
Step 4: *Inventory*	Step 10: *Truthful*
Step 5: *Honest*	Step 11: *Prayer*
Step 6: *Ready*	Step 12: *Awakening*

These words can be written alongside of each of the 12 steps on the runner. The words can also be inscribed down each side of the mirror with a permanent marker. Use your imagination and enter this ritual with a reverence for the transforming powers of the recovery process.

13
Inner Mapping

Within each of us is a wellspring of wisdom and awareness waiting to help us guide our lives so that we are empowered to make a difference in the world. But even those people aware of the existence of this knowledge sometimes have a hard time accessing it. We know that this source of infinite wisdom lives in us, but where is it? How do we find it? If only we had a road map to show us the way.

This ritual does just that. Through the creative process it calls upon our deepest thoughts and emotions to create an Inner Map of images, metaphors and symbols to guide us through our personal evolution. Once the process has begun, it is like a snowball rolling downhill — it becomes so powerful, it is nearly impossible to stop.

YOU'LL NEED

Scissors; glue; construction paper; markers; and old magazines that can be cut up.

THE RITUAL

Ask each person to reflect briefly on an aspect of their life that they wish to focus on for growth, guidance and understanding. Because our minds are much more receptive to images, have each person cut out pictures and symbols, as well as words, to represent a particular area of life. The next step is to arrange these images and words on the construction paper. Together, this collage of thoughts, feelings and desires forms a visual Inner Map, leading us deep into our hearts and souls — to our very essence.

Through designing and sharing our Inner Map, we creatively participate in inviting new images, metaphors, and symbols to guide us in our evolution. The word metaphor comes from the Greek and literally means "to carry over."

A metaphor is a figure of speech — an implied comparison in which a word or phrase ordinarily used to describe one thing is applied to another. An example of a metaphor would be, "All the world is a stage." Metaphors can help us in allowing the images and words to "carry over" important messages for our emotional growth. One woman used the metaphor of a pregnant woman ready to give birth on her Inner Map to symbolize her rebirth after the end of a bad marriage. Another woman used a picture of a child by a stream to represent the space she was creating in her life for play, relaxation and inner reflection. A man placed a big snowflake on his Inner Map to reflect the unique qualities and newly discovered dimensions of his life.

This experience, which taps into our inner realm of wisdom and guidance, is not the same as "Treasure Mapping," which is often used by those seeking material gain. Inner mapping brings forth spiritual and mental growth. The images come like dreams to transform our lives and bring in renewed vitality. The Inner Mapping experience is a powerful tool to guide people to a new awareness and wisdom that is their essence. After the process has begun, most people find that they begin to see images and symbols that are metaphors for their lives. Spontaneously, they are guided to find just the right pictures to add to their Inner Maps. These images and symbols become like little stepping stones to our inner world, guiding our lives with powerful pictures that can tell an entire story about our experiences. Life is an incredible adventure that unfolds each day. Inner Mapping helps us to understand that sacred story by providing guiding images and metaphors for the journey.

The Inner Map can be put up in the home or workplace as a reminder of what is happening in our lives and the avenues that we would like to explore in our emotional evolution.

WHO CAN USE THE RITUAL

Individuals . . . The Inner Map can reflect a person's internal promises. By finding pictures that represent the promise to themselves, they are reinforcing their commitment to carrying them out. Perhaps the person has made a commitment to inner spiritual growth. They may look for images to guide them to better eating and exercise habits. The images can be the guide to a new way of life.

Families . . . The Inner Mapping experience is a delightful way to enhance communication and bring the family closer together. Each member of the family can visualize images that reflect the family experience such as love, communication, togetherness and fun. When changes occur in the family, such as a move to a new area, an Inner Map can provide a bridge of pictures and images to the new community. Often children find this very reassuring as the family joins together to create a visual map of the transition. The group creation of the map can build a solid bond within the family. Put up your Inner Maps in a prominent place so they can regularly fill your minds and spirits with guiding images.

Therapists . . . Inner Mapping can be an insightful process of looking at the story of one's life in terms of the seasons. Spring is infancy and childhood; summer, the youth, teen and young adult years; fall, the middle adult, career and family years; and winter is the mature adult who has new life opportunities, new interests and life goals.

Have the group section off their large piece of construction paper into quadrants and place images and symbols within them for each of the seasons of life. If they have not reached some of the later stages, have them imagine what those seasons might be like.

Sharing can take place in pairs after the process is complete. Afterwards, the group as a whole may want to share the significant insights they had while doing the Inner Mapping.

Inner Mapping also works well with individuals or families going through major life transitions such as divorce and the death of a loved one.

The idea of a wholesale life change can be frightening. Many people literally freeze with the fear of not knowing which way to go. They are suddenly in uncharted territory. Inner Mapping can help these people chart a course for the future by asking them to think about how they would like to see their lives evolve. The focus becomes dreaming and planning rather than anxiously questioning what will happen next.

Suggest that the client choose pictures and symbols that reflect the new way of life as it is emerging, such as finding pictures of a new home or a happy family. After they have completed the Inner Map, have them bring it to the session to share with you or the group. Children generally do well expressing themselves this way.

Spiritual Leaders . . . The Inner Mapping is a wonderful way to awaken spirituality, by focusing on the image, symbols and metaphors of divinity in our day-to-day existence. The Inner Map could reflect the different aspects of God within and all around us. One woman created her vision of the cosmic mother, reflecting the beauty of the earth and all creation.

In the Christian tradition, Lent is a time for releasing and cleansing. Whenever something is cleaned out, it is wise to put something better in its place. During Lent, the Inner Map can be used to fill up the soul with images of blessing, healing and harmony. Representations of spiritual development and growth can adorn the Inner Map.

Youth groups can use Inner Mapping as a way to discover some of the aspects of the inner self, and to connect their spirituality in practical ways to their daily life experiences.

Inner Mapping works well as a retreat experience that can be shared in groups, mapping out one's spiritual quest. One person put seeds in various stages of growth, taking root, as a visual image of her spiritual quest. At each stage she was the gardener attending to the new growth, watering, weeding and nurturing her own spiritual blossoming.

The process is a great way to create images for guiding the spiritual community in its collective growth and evolution. The images can represent the qualities the spiritual community wishes to see manifest such as cooperation, forgiveness, generosity, teamwork, compassion and vitality.

Recovery Groups . . . People in recovery need guiding images and metaphors to help in the ongoing battle for sobriety. Images evoking a strong internal response can powerfully guide the recovering person where words often fall short. One man used the image of a Mack truck, saying that nothing was going to stop him on this road of recovery.

Ask the group or individual to see images of what their life will be like without using drugs, alcohol, or engaging in other compulsive behavior. What symbols will carry them through this day? Ask them to allow an image of something very significant to appear before their mind's eye that would stop them from relapse or using that substance or behavior again. After they have created their Inner Maps, have them share in pairs or in small groups what they have constructed and the guiding images that are important to their recovery. Be sure to have them put the Inner Map up in a prominent place so they can see it daily.

Teachers . . . The Inner Map can visually express each student's journey through school. Positive images and symbols can increase the students' sense of self-esteem. Discussion can take place about the idea of metaphor, including questions such as: How do metaphors guide us in life? What are some examples of people in history who were guided by a metaphor? What metaphor is guiding your life experience? The Inner Map can creatively reflect a guiding metaphor for their life experience.

14
A Life
Remembered

The purpose of this ritual is to offer some options for the way we take part in memorial and funeral services. When a loved one dies, grief often prevents those who had been close to them from thinking rationally. In this very vulnerable time, people often spend considerable amounts of money on unnecessary, elaborate funeral arrangements, thinking that this is the best way to honor the memory of the deceased. The creation of the ritual is often taken away from the people who need to create it the most — the family — and handed over to the funeral director who "manages" the affair. The result is a service that is often abbreviated, not allowing those present to remember the person more fully and deal with their own grief. It is our belief that we can best honor those who have died by giving their surviving loved ones more control over the arrangements through a true memorial service in which everyone can keep the person's memory alive through the telling of their life story — A Life Remembered.

YOU'LL NEED

A picture of the person who has died; a Bible; a stuffed heart; and a talking stick, rain stick or other item that could be passed from person to person.

THE RITUAL

A Life Remembered, in which all those close to the deceased share their remembrances together, is one theme recommended instead of the traditional obituary and funeral service. The service was inspired by the life and death of a beloved storyteller named Lillian Muyia. This group sharing is best done in a church, home or community setting where time is not a problem. Everyone who wishes to share should be given the opportunity to do so. Although this type of memorial service can and has been done meaningfully in funeral homes, funeral directors often want the service concluded in about one hour.

At the memorial service, invite people to share personal remembrances of the person's life — stories of times together, the spirit that made that person special and unique, accomplishments that touched people's lives, the influence the person had on their family, friends, community and church. A picture of the person is often set up in front of the gathering. The leader can begin with an invocation, prayer, or reading, and then start the sharing with, "I want to tell the story of _____." After the leader has shared remembrances, an item such as the person's Bible, a small stuffed heart or a talking stick can be passed around the room or up front to the next speaker. The leader can prompt the story by asking, "Who would like to continue the story of _____?" The Bible, heart or talking stick can be passed from person to person as the life story is shared. Children are often the most precious in sharing their innocent thoughts and should be supported in speaking what is in their hearts to share. The stories can be taped on audio or video cassette and given to the family as a personal gift from the hearts of family and friends.

The sharing is a reminder to all that as long as we are alive, the person continues to live on within our memories. We are all the keepers of their never-ending story. The soul continues its eternal journey, and the life we shared lives on in all involved.

Sometimes we close the sharing by quoting or singing the chorus of the old hymn, "I Love To Tell The Story."

The service can also take place in a garden setting. Some churches and other groups have planted "Gardens of Love" in memory of loved ones and friends who have died. Plants, trees and flowers are added to the garden in the memory of a person's life. The community makes a commitment to tend the garden. It also serves as a living sanctuary where people can work through their grief and talk to the loved one in their own way. Sometimes names are placed in areas around the garden. Benches and chairs are often donated in the name of a loved one. Ashes can also be sprinkled in the garden if the person wished.

TRANSFORMATION STORY (FROM GAY)

This is a story about a loving couple named Sadie and John. They had been married for over 40 years when John suddenly had a massive stroke. From the time they first met, Sadie and John were inseparable.

David and I went to the hospital to see them both. Sadie stood by John's bed, holding his hand as he lay still in a deep coma. We all joined hands and touched John's hands as we prayed together. During the prayer a vivid, dream-like image came to me of John standing in the middle of a tunnel. John could not come out of the tunnel at either end. I did not say anything until we got out to the car. I told David of the image and my concern that John was unable to return or to move on. I wondered if we should talk with Sadie. David suggested that we continue to pray about it and see what happened in the next few days.

Sadie called a few days later to tell us that John had died. She said, "Right before the hospital called I was in the basement doing some wash. I felt John's presence close by me. I vividly imagined him standing right in front of me and I held him in my arms. I said, 'It's okay if you need to go, John. I will be alright.'" Sadie wept softly. As I listened to Sadie tell what happened, I, too, was flooded with emotions as I remembered the tunnel John was now able to go through, at just the right time, in just the right way. Sadie continued, "It wasn't more than an hour later that the hospital called and said that I should come. I knew right away that John had died."

This beautiful story of eternal love and tenderness was shared as part of John's memorial service. Telling it helped us all remember that there is an interconnectedness that neither coma nor death ends. Our relationships are at a soul level, and while many other things pass away, our relationships never end. Sadie and John lived this, and we all shared in it by the telling of their story.

WHO CAN USE THE RITUAL

Families . . . A Life Remembered can work with any type of funeral arrangement. It can start the healing by honoring the loss and giving people permission to share some of what is held inside. Sometimes people think that sharing their feelings and stories only makes things worse. But in fact, just the opposite is true. We need to share our stories because they are the glue that holds families together. What would a family be without its stories? Stories form the framework for a family's existence by communicating its values, love, strengths, struggles, hurts and triumphs. The greatest gift we give to each other is the telling of our stories — a living tapestry carried from one generation to the next.

Therapists . . . This ritual works well in helping individuals or families to process grief. One of the most restorative acts is telling the stories, sometimes over and over, of the person's life. This is an important part of the healing process and needs to be honored with patience and love.

Spiritual Leaders . . . A Life Remembered is a meaningful ceremony that will long be remembered by all who take part. Often after this kind of sharing, people leave saying, "That was the best memorial service I have ever seen; I really felt that we honored my mother by telling her story." The process allows the minister to help the living celebrate the life story of the deceased. All the attention and load is not placed on the minister to carry the whole service.

Teachers . . . Sometimes children die. When they do we need to honor them and give those children remaining in the classroom a way to share their feelings. A Life Remembered gives children a bridge to cross, a means to tell their stories and a chance to honor the death of a fellow student.

(This could also apply if a teacher dies.) Poems, artwork and other creative projects could assist the students in expressing their grief. A tree or flowers can be planted on the school grounds in memory of the student's life.

15
Crossing-Over Ritual

In the Christian tradition, Good Friday is the commemoration of the day when Jesus died and was buried. It precedes the greatest day of the Christian year, Easter, the celebration of His resurrection. To believers, this signified that there is a life everlasting and gave hope to all for salvation, a crossing over into a new life. The Crossing-Over Ritual offers a creative, participatory ceremony for Good Friday services. The purpose is for people to see themselves in a new way by crossing the bridge to a better life while letting the old way of living or behaving pass away, thus helping to create a better world for everyone.

YOU'LL NEED

A bridge that people can cross or a facsimile of one; soft music; and plenty of tissue for overflowing emotions.

THE RITUAL

This ritual includes the "Car Wash" Ceremony tunnel as described in Chapter 19 (see page 135). Before the ceremony begins, form this tunnel at the far end of the bridge with a few people who will take their turn crossing the bridge when everyone else has finished.

Begin with a brief meditation on the topic of Good Friday to help set the mood for the crossing over. Ask people to concentrate on the limiting behaviors or thoughts they would like to release from their lives. Examples are fear, doubt, lack of trust or faith, procrastination, and long-held resentments. As a part of the meditation include the following directions:

Each of us will have the opportunity to come forward and, before crossing the bridge, speak to one person. Say what you would like to release in your thoughts that will help you to experience life more fully here and now.

People will be at the foot of the bridge who will lovingly listen as you share what you want to release. After you have finished, cross the bridge and walk over into a new understanding of what it means to be more fully alive and fulfilled in life.

On the other side of the bridge, you will be greeted by the voices of love and affirmation. Receive the words of love, welcome and affirmation they have for you. Simply close your eyes, hold your hands in front of you in an open and receptive way, and walk slowly. Hands will lovingly guide you through a passageway welcoming you into new life. Allow yourself to take in and feel the love and acceptance there is for you here and now. Allow yourself to be guided through the two lines of people that form the welcoming committee into this new consciousness. After you have received the welcome from others, you then become part of the line and welcome those who follow you.

End the meditation. Instruct people again as to what they are expected to do and have them form a line and participate in the Crossing-Over Ritual.

Conclude the experience with a prayer, song or reading of a poem or passage from the Bible.

WHO CAN USE THE RITUAL

Spiritual Leaders . . . This spiritual experience can be adapted and used for any service, retreat or class setting. We first utilized the Crossing-Over Ritual as a Good Friday service. Now it has become a highly successful part of our annual spiritual journey together. In a real sense the crucifixion and resurrection were crossing-over experiences that Jesus shared with us as living examples of our own overcoming power. Looked at in this way, Jesus acted as a bridge builder. Now we need to cross the bridge, not just revere the bridge builder.

This ritual can accommodate hundreds of people. We have had over 500 people participate. Any size group over 20 can benefit spiritually by crossing the bridge together into greater understanding. Be sure to allow plenty of time to complete the crossing so everyone who wants to can participate.

It is truly amazing to see how patient people are as they wait to cross the bridge, spending time in thoughtful prayer or just sitting quietly listening to the background music.

In our experience, we found that each person who crossed the bridge was deeply touched by the vibrant spiritual energy that we evoked in those hours together. It reminded us all to walk the path with Jesus and cross into greater understanding of our oneness and divinity.

16
Candle-Lighting Ceremonies

The use of fire was critical to human evolution. By learning to develop and control it, humans were able to cook, make heat and light, construct tools and clay pots and clear land for farming. Civilizations developed based on the ability to smelt and form metals. Fire has always been worshipped by humans for its beneficial uses when controlled and its awesome power in nature. It has been central to many religions — symbolic of God, home and family, purification, immortality and renewal. Perhaps because it is so deeply ingrained in our history and evolution, the dancing flames of a fire appear mystical and sacred. Candle-lighting ceremonies which use the power of fire, can be moving, powerful experiences to commemorate special occasions such as a graduation or holiday.

YOU'LL NEED

Candles; matches; candle holders; and salt or sand trays.

THE RITUAL

There are several different variations of the Candle-Lighting Ceremony:

Graduation Candle-Lighting Ceremony

A Candle-Lighting Ceremony can be a meaningful culmination to a graduation ceremony. The Center for Humanistic Studies incorporates candle lighting into their graduation by having students light candles as they walk up on stage to take their diplomas. As they light their candles, they complete the statement, "I light this candle in honor of . . ." or "I light this candle as a symbol of . . ." Each student takes about one minute to reflect on their graduate school experience. This is a nice touch to the ceremony because it allows

111

students to share their rite of passage through stories of their mutual growth and struggles.

Spiritual Healing Candle-Lighting Ceremony

Gay leads a weekend women's retreat called Spirit Healer. A part of the retreat is a 12-hour silence beginning at about 10:00 p.m. and lasting until 10:00 a.m. The silence closes with the Candle-Lighting Ceremony. Each woman lights her candle in front of the entire group, completing the statement, "I light this candle in honor of . . ." or "I light this candle as a symbol of . . ." Participants find this is a powerful release of the energy collected in the rite of silence. Burning candles become a visual symbol of the flame of life that illuminates our hearts and heals us at our innermost level.

Family Candle-Lighting Ceremony

This activity can take place in any community, church or large family gathering. Our church has a Family Fun Night when children and parents bring sleeping bags and stay all night. The evening includes games, pizza and a pretend campfire. We fill a large metal tub with sand and insert a candle for each child and parent. Each child and adult lights a candle in our pretend campfire. As the candles are lit, each person has the opportunity to share a thought on "What my family means to me." They complete statements such as: "My family is special because . . ." or "I like being in my family because . . ." After everyone shares their special thoughts we all snuggle up around the campfire of candles, sing songs and tell stories. The evening is always a great success.

Christmas Candle-Lighting Ceremony

Christmas is celebrated in our church with a Christmas Candle-Lighting Service. As each person enters the sanctuary, they are given a four-inch-long candle. Every candle has a Bible verse wrapped around its base, which is then held on with a small rubber band. We type out hundreds of different verses for the candles. Each year people come in droves to see which verse they will receive. The verse often becomes a theme for the year and a guidance to each receiver. The ushers remind people to remove their verses before they walk up front where they light their candle from a large candle, representing Christ's light, and place it in one of the large trays filled with salt. Each candle placed in the tray stands up next to all the others, forming a bright block of light.

Traditional Christmas songs are then sung together, and the congregation unites in a prayerful lighting of 12 candles representing spiritual qualities they would like to affirm in their lives. There is an outer lighting of the candles and a meditation process that is entered into together. The meditation process begins with the facilitator saying each line, then the congregation repeating it in unison, with a brief silence following each candle lighting. The meditation is as follows:

Before God's holy altar within me, I light my light of Faith.

Before God's holy altar within me, I light my light of Strength.

Before God's holy altar within me, I light my light of Wisdom.

Before God's holy altar within me, I light my light of Love.

Before God's holy altar within me, I light my light of Power.

Before God's holy altar within me, I light my light of Imagination.

Before God's holy altar within me, I light my light of Understanding.

Before God's holy altar within me, I light my light of Willingness.

Before God's holy altar within me, I light my light of Divine Order.

Before God's holy altar within me, I light my light of Enthusiasm.

Before God's holy altar within me, I light my light of Freedom.

Before God's holy altar within me, I light my light of Life.

We remind everyone:

You have placed your candle in a bed of salt. There it is shining and adding its brightness to the illumination of the world. The bed of salt represents the earth and all creation, for we are indeed the salt of the earth and one with the creative life process. Here at the altar of your own heart you lit your candle of prayer. This light represents a new birth of Spirit within you. Walk lovingly, respecting all life, using wisely the powers you have been given. Walk serenely in the light of the Christ love.

Conclude with a group song or chant such as "Silent Night," holding hands in a room brightened only by candlelight.

Candle Lighting For Introduction

This ceremony is designed to help people get to know each other in a group setting. Have people gather into groups of four and give each individual a candle. Begin the ritual with some kind of opening or invocation appropriate for the group and this occasion. Play soft background music. Ask people to take their lit candle around the room, silently walking and stopping occasionally to make eye contact with others. Have them reflect for a moment on the spark, inner light and radiance they see in the eyes of each person. If they choose, they can exchange their candles with each other. After about 10 minutes, have everyone return to their small groups and share some of the feelings and thoughts that came to them as they participated in this ritual.

WHO CAN USE THE RITUAL

Individuals . . . Candle-lighting ceremonies can be done alone or with one other person to honor new insight, illumination and guidance received from a dream or from life experience. Lighting candles is a wonderful way to create "sacred space." Notice how lighting a candle can instantly change the feeling or energy in a room. Writing by candlelight is inspiring and special. As a couple, we often light many candles as a way to honor the sacred space of our lovemaking. Taking a bath by candle light is a sacred pleasure. Be creative and let candles be a delightful expression of your spirit.

Families . . . We join with our family at different times of the year to have our own, personal Candle-Lighting Ceremony. Sometimes we spontaneously speak what is in our hearts to one another. On birthdays, in addition to the usual ceremony of making a wish before blowing out the candles, we have also asked everyone around the table to light a candle for the birthday person and share their special wish or blessing for them. Each place setting has a candle and holder by it so that the candles illumine the table after the wishes are shared.

Therapists . . . Can use the Graduation Candle-Lighting Ceremony to conclude some part of the group experience, affirming that each member of the group is moving forward, graduating to the next level of life experience. The Family Candle-Lighting Ceremony can be used to help families express thoughts of love and appreciation to one another. The Candle-Lighting For Introduction can help people get to know one another at a deep level through non-verbal interaction that includes a group experience.

Spiritual Leaders . . . Members of the clergy can use all of the ceremonies listed for retreat and group experiences. The Christmas Candle-Lighting Ceremony is a special service celebrated in the Christian community and can be adapted to fit into many other spiritual communities.

The Candle-Lighting Ceremony can also be focused on the energy of the feminine aspects of God and our soul connection to Mother Earth. Words such as water, fire, earth, air, giver of life, fountain of energy, beauty and love can reflect our understanding that the "She" nurtures and sustains us all.

The Candle-Lighting Ceremony can also include passages from the extensive literature of wisdom in the Hebrew scriptures. The light of wisdom in the poetry of those scriptures often refers to the divine in us as a "she." Remarkably, in a male-dominated world, we find a celebration of transformative wisdom as Sophia (Wisdom), bringing light and goodness forth into our lives. Here is how Wisdom is described in the Book of Wisdom, adapted from The New Jerusalem Bible:

Within her is a spirit intelligent, holy,
unique, manifold, subtle,
active, incisive, unsullied,
lucid, invulnerable, benevolent, insightful,
irresistible, beneficent, loving to humankind,

steadfast, dependable, unperturbed,
almighty, all-surveying,
penetrating all intelligent, pure
and most subtle spirits;
for Wisdom is quicker to move than any motion;
she is so pure, she pervades and permeates all things.
She is a breath of the power of God,
pure emanation of the glory of the Almighty;
and nothing impure can find a way into her.
She is a reflection of the eternal light,
untarnished mirror of God's active power,
image of God's goodness.

Wisdom 7:22-26

She is indeed more splendid than the sun,
she outshines all the constellations;
compared with light, she takes first place,
for light must yield to night,
but against Wisdom evil cannot prevail.
Strongly she reaches from one end of the world to the other
and she governs the whole world for its good.

Wisdom 7:29 — 8:1

Recovery Groups . . . Use a Candle-Lighting Ceremony
to celebrate sobriety anniversaries. It is also a good way to
introduce new people into a group. The 12 candles can be
symbolic of the recognition of the 12 steps in recovery. Steps
one through 12 can be summarized with the following words
as each candle is lit: admitted, believe, decision, inventory,
honesty, ready, humble, willing, amendments, truthful, prayer
and awakening. A brief silence follows the lighting of each
candle. Have a special prayer and silence at the end for all
those who are still sick and suffering with addictions.

Teachers . . . The Graduation Candle-Lighting Ceremony
is best used as a year-end ceremony that each class can
participate in individually.

17
Energizing Name Ritual

As discussed in Chapter Six (White Stone Ritual), our name plays an important role in defining our identity. Choosing a new, spiritual name is a powerful way to affirm qualities within ourselves that we would like to express. The Energizing Name Ritual gives people the opportunity to do that with group reinforcement, and also serves as a way for participants to get to know one another.

YOU'LL NEED

Name tags and pens or markers.

THE RITUAL

This must me done in small groups of no more than four or five people. Larger groups can be divided accordingly. The TR experience takes place in two parts:

Part 1: Spiritual Name

Begin by leading the whole group in a time of reflection:

Close your eyes and let yourself relax. Reflect for a time on where your name came from. Did it come from your parents? How do you feel about your name? Does it fit you? Meditate for a few minutes on the question, "Who am I?" What comes forth in your mind as you ask this question? Is it a name? A quality? An affirmation of your own uniqueness? Maybe it is a descriptive word with the same letter as your first name, such as "powerful Pat."

Use this name as your first name or your middle name. Sometimes a spiritual teacher gives you a name. Giving a spiritual name has been a long-standing tradition in many cultures: African, Asian, Native American and Hebrew. Jacob became Israel after he wrestled with the angel. Jesus gave Simon his new name — Peter, the rock. Saul became Paul after his conversion experience which started on the road to Damascus.

Let a spiritual name come to you; think of the qualities you would like to express through this name.
(Pause for a time of silence.)

After a few minutes, conclude the meditation and have the group write their spiritual names with a marker in large print on a name tag and put it on. Ask them each to share briefly with the group the meaning of their spiritual names. Give them some time to conclude the sharing, then ask people to stand in small circles joining hands.

Part 2: Energizing Our Name

Demonstrate this process with one group so all can see how it takes place.

1. Form a group of four or five.
2. Hold hands, left hand palm up, right hand palm down, to open up the energy flow. Stay silent for a few minutes.
3. One person gets in the middle of the circle. Outside people each rub hands together a few times.
4. Cup hands over the person in the middle, bringing in the energy of the sky. Visualize raindrops sprinkling all around them. The person in the middle should take energy into every area of their body, especially any areas that need healing.
5. Now outside people take the energy from the earth, sweeping upward with their hands beginning at the person's feet. Repeat the focus person's spiritual name over and over as energy is transferred up their entire body. Outside people shake hands off when they are finished. Let the person in the middle have time to savor the energy for a moment before re-entering the outer circle. Repeat the process with each person.

Who Can Use the Ritual

Families . . . It is wonderful to share with children the history of their names. For our family, this ritual is a bonding and sharing experience that helps our children on the path to self-knowledge and self-actualization. The insight and affirmation in sharing our spiritual name helped to heighten the atmosphere of trust and understanding.

Therapists . . . This ritual works well as an introductory group experience. It is especially effective if the counselor is working from a spiritual as well as psychological perspective. The concept of spiritual names is not specific to one belief. Perhaps some discussion could take place concerning the difference between working with the spiritual realm and religious beliefs. The spiritual perspective transcends the creeds and dogmas of specific religions.

Spiritual Leaders . . . Retreats, classes and special services can be greatly enhanced with this enlightening experience. A brief discussion of Biblical name changes could precede the sharing of the ritual.

Recovery Groups . . . The spiritual realm, as reflected in the idea of a Higher Power, is an important factor in the recovery movement. A spiritual name is effective as a reminder of a new life and connection to God or a "power within."

18
Phoenix Rising Ritual

Life is a process. Sometimes we move forward, sometimes backward and sometimes we just stand still. Arguably, being stuck is the most frustrating of the three options, for stagnation tends to make people feel trapped and without options. Although we can become imprisoned by situations over which we have no control, often certain behaviors contribute to our lack of freedom, including procrastination, worry and fear. Still, people are afraid to give up these habitual behaviors for a better life because of their fear of the unknown.

This ritual uses the image of the mythological Egyptian bird, the phoenix, rising renewed from the flames, to help people gain greater freedom in their lives. Although it was designed to complement the Christian celebration of Lent, it can be adapted and used in a variety of settings to help people shed something limiting or unproductive on the way to gaining personal freedom.

YOU'LL NEED

"Phoenix medallions" (see ordering information in Appendix B); and medium-point permanent ink markers or inexpensive electric engravers can be purchased and shared. The engraving process makes inscriptions more permanent.

THE RITUAL

Everyone is given a Phoenix medallion as they enter the room. The ritual begins with a meditation as each person reflects on the medallion's image of the phoenix and the words below it, "And still I rise," inspired by the poet Maya Angelou.

The meditation can go as follows:

Relax into this time of meditation. In your own mind silently speak words of peace and relaxation, such as, "peace, be still, peace be still."
(Pause)

Let your body lovingly respond to your words and thoughts of peace and relaxation. Notice your breathing and with each breath feel your body becoming more and more relaxed.
(Pause)

See in your mind's eye the phoenix which is on the medallion you have received today. The phoenix comes from Egyptian mythology. The miraculous bird was the embodiment of the Sun God. According to legend, the bird lived for 500 years and then burned itself to ash on a pyre. But the bird did not die; it rose in youthful freshness to live again. The phoenix is often used as a symbol of immortality. Let this bird remind you now of your winged, transcendent self — the part of you that is immortal. You, as the phoenix, are a miraculous being. You, as the phoenix, can rise from the ashes to the freedom and freshness of new life.

It is from the powerful presence within you and all around you that you are transformed. You are the creation clothed in flesh. All freedom begins with your awareness and conscious connection to the transcendent within you. The thoughts held in your mind at this moment are providing that connection.
(Pause)

In every one of us there are thoughts and feelings that keep us from experiencing freedom and our conscious contact with inner wisdom. Let come to your mind some of what you may want or need to let go of so that you can rise out of these ashes. Some of these ashes may be insecurity, anger, guilt, perfectionism, worry, procrastination, envy, impatience, blame, indecision or jealousy. These are normal to feel on occasion, but any of them in excess can begin to limit and consume your life energies. In your thoughts, briefly

reflect on what behaviors you would like to turn to ash and rise from, renewed.
(Pause)

Affirm in your own mind, "My winged self transcends and overcomes even the most difficult or long-term problems." (Repeat this slowly again.) "I rise as the Phoenix out of the ashes to new freedom."
(Pause)

Now, let come to your mind in the next moments of silence a word or two that are symbols of your freedom. Let come to your mind a word or two that symbolize your transformation. These words will be written on the back of your phoenix medallion with permanent marking pens that will be provided for you. Let words such as acceptance, generosity, faith, humility, trust, forgiveness, love, patience, praise, honesty, action, self-reliance, laughter, life, order, strength, truth and spiritual awakening come to your mind. Be guided to the word or words that best describe the qualities you would like to express. Let the words come to you in the next moments of silence.
(Pause)

Remember the words, keep them in your mind and say them to yourself now several times.
(Pause)

Following the meditation, you will receive a special pen to write your words on the back of your phoenix medallion. Carry your medallion with you each day in your pocket, purse or wallet. Look at it often and contemplate the phrase inscribed on it, "And still I rise." Each day is another opportunity to know your freedom, to rise again. Let us say this together, "And still I rise." (Repeat together.)
(Pause)

Now take a moment to feel that power moving through you from the tips of your toes to the top of your head.
(Pause)

Know that when you open your eyes the transformation will have begun in you.

Following the meditation, circulate the permanent ink markers throughout the group and have each person write their personal words on the back of their phoenix medallion.

WHO CAN USE THE RITUAL

Therapists . . . The ritual can be used anytime as a group process to help people gain a greater sense of personal freedom. Include a discussion of how some excessive and compulsive ways of thinking can consume our natural life energy and creativity. The phoenix medallion can be carried by group members as a reminder of their commitment to inner growth.

Spiritual Leaders . . . This is a good Ash Wednesday ritual during the first week of Lent. We have used the following additions to the meditation text which has already been suggested:

In our spiritual community, our focus is on Jesus and rising into the Christ consciousness of freedom and oneness of all life. Jesus showed us, beyond a doubt, that we are more than our minds and bodies. We are spiritual beings clothed in a beautiful body with a wonderful creative mind. It is through this powerful connection of the mind, body and spirit that we are transformed. This is the time to prepare for our celebration of resurrection. In order to do this we must let go of limitations so that we may realize more fully the God power within and all around us. Lent is observed as our 40 days to new freedom.

We also had our Sunday school and youth groups involved and made the language appropriate for the concerns and maturity level of each age group. For example, with the younger children we suggested rising out of the ashes of unkindness, lying and feelings of unimportance.

Recovery Groups . . . The phoenix medallion is also a symbol of rising into a powerful sense of freedom in recovery. The medallion can be carried as a reminder to those in recovery of rising out of the ashes of addiction into the freedom of a new life. The affirmation we like to include as part of the meditation is, "I am Higher Powered." We often remind people in recovery "that we alone do it, but we never do it alone." The phoenix is our reminder of that part of us that is "Higher Powered." Each day is a new opportunity to rise again into this awareness.

TRANSFORMATION STORY

Concern ran through a young mother's mind as she learned that her teenage son had been skipping school and making failing grades. A recommendation was made to place him in the "at risk" program at his high school. The mother prayed daily that God would direct and guide her son. On Easter, she gave him a phoenix medallion and told him of her belief that he could rise above all the difficulties he was facing.

Because of his problems, the boy was put in the school's "at risk" program, created for troubled youths on the verge of dropping out. Each year students in the program choose a symbol or emblem for the year. It becomes a motto for their class — to call them to a higher purpose, to give them strength and courage to be themselves and to succeed. All of the students are asked to participate in designing a symbol and finding a motto that will collectively inspire them. The young man, inspired by the phoenix medallion his mother gave him, drew a large rendition of it and included the slogan from the coin, "And Still I Rise." He found the poem by Maya Angelou, from which the slogan had been inspired, and read it to his classmates.

The teenagers listened and then took the final vote. There were three emblems that had made it into the final count. With the votes counted and everyone waiting, the announcement was made: "The winning motto is, 'And Still I Rise' with the Phoenix as our new emblem."

The young man stood in awe. This was the first time in his life he had ever won anything. The affirmation from his own peer group inspired him in a way that truly transformed his life. He was an agent for change in this group, and for the first time he had a sense of his own contribution to a higher calling and a greater purpose in life.

The boy's mother was radiant as she shared this story with Gay, saying that her son's attendance in school was no longer a problem and that his grades were steadily improving. She embraced Gay and thanked her for designing the medallion. She purchased medallions for each of the teens, so that every day they would be reminded of the transcendent spirit alive within each of them. Each class member signed their name around the large picture of the phoenix which hung in the hallway by their classroom. "And Still I Rise" was the motto that carried them into a new experience of themselves and life!

Later, Gay heard from another teacher whose elementary school students had received low scores after taking their scholastic exams. The teachers and administration had knocked themselves out preparing the children, but the school as a whole scored much lower than they had anticipated. Morale hit an all time low.

This teacher had received one of the phoenix medallions and carried it in her pocket daily, reminding herself that there was no situation in her school or classroom that she could not rise above. In an effort to change the mood at her school, she purchased a medallion for each adult. She also drew a large rendition of the phoenix and posted it at the entrance to the school building. The collective outlook shifted from disappointment to determination as the educators took a moment to look at their personal medallion every day and affirm in their own minds, "And Still We Rise." The thoughtfulness of that teacher lifted the level of consciousness of the whole school.

19
"Car Wash"
Ceremony

Just as cars are used to transport us from place to place, our bodies are our souls' vehicles of transportation. From time to time, our bodies need to be "washed" with gentle strokes of love and appreciation. The "Car Wash" Ceremony affirms our love and support of one another as physical and spiritual beings.

We have tried to think of a more elegant name for this ceremony but it seems to continue to be known simply as "The Car Wash." People of all ages have responded enthusiastically to this ceremony. We often use it in combination with other rituals or as a closing ceremony after a retreat or workshop.

YOU'LL NEED

Soft, meditative background music.

THE RITUAL

Depending on the size of the group, The Car Wash can be done in two different ways:

1. *Groups of 50 and under:* Form two equal lines of people, facing one another about an arm's length apart. This passageway of people is a tunnel of love. Have someone at the beginning of the passageway help each person begin their walk through the tunnel of people. This person reminds the people walking through the passageway to walk slowly, eyes closed, hands outstretched. As they slowly walk through the tunnel, people will gently take their hands and guide them through the passage and lovingly stroke their backs, whispering softly in their ears words of appreciation and praise appropriate to the group. Suggestions of things to be said are: "You are God's beloved"; "You are so loved"; "You are special"; "I am so glad you are part

of my life"; and "You are so appreciated." Recovery group members may want to affirm to one another, with "You are God-powered" or "You are an overcomer," and make it specific to their particular needs.

Once a person reaches the end of the passageway, they become part of the tunnel of love and praise all of those who follow them. The process is repeated until everyone has had a chance to go through the tunnel.

2. *Groups of more than 50 people:* Ask about 20 or more people to come up and form the initial Car Wash passageway. The rest of the group can line up and pass through the tunnel of love and praise. Those who pass through become a part of the passageway. After everyone has passed through, the initial 20 people can go through, one at a time, following each other and slowly walking and receiving their showering of love and blessings. Be sure there is sufficient room for the Car Wash to bend around corners and spread out enough to accommodate the entire group. We have performed this ceremony with as many as 500 people. If necessary, two or more Car Wash lines can be in operation at the same time.

WHO CAN USE THE RITUAL

Therapists . . . This is a wonderful group experience of support, sharing, appreciation and personal love for others. This can be used as a culminating ceremony or rite of passage.

Spiritual Leaders . . . Can be used in a retreat, a class or as part of Sunday worship to affirm one another and share the healing touch. This spiritually uplifting experience can be used in conjunction with other rituals. Appropriate for all ages and as a celebration of rite of passage in the church community.

Recovery Groups . . . Reinforces the support group system and works very well as a special ceremony or on graduation.

20
Mother's Day
Or Father's Day
Ceremony

Down through the ages, older generations have passed their acquired wisdom down to younger generations. Older generations, too, learn from the spirit and vitality of younger generations. We are all interdependent with one another as we keep learning in life. Still, the much touted "generation gap" sometimes prevents us from doing this. A way to bridge this gap is to celebrate Mother's Day or Father's Day with a ceremony that includes a time of sharing and inter-generational blessing.

YOU'LL NEED

Any size group of willing men and women.

THE RITUAL

In our spiritual community, on Mother's Day and again on Father's Day, we celebrate this inter-generational ceremony. The same, essential process is used for both men and women.

First, two pairs of women from different generations are asked to model the way to participate in this ceremony. Each stands facing the other. We refer to all the women over 50 years of age as the "grand women" — an appropriate title for those we look up to for their maturity and wisdom. All the women under 50 are referred to as the "younger women."

The grand women stand first. The rest of the group lifts up their hands, with arms extended, and gives the grand women a special acknowledgment spoken by one person representing everyone. Tell them of your appreciation for their part in keeping the community and its families alive, well and whole.

Ask the younger women to stand and pair up with one of the grand women. Mothers and daughters may stand together, but it is not a requirement. At this point, the grand women should place their hands on the younger women's shoulders and verbalize thoughts of love, blessings or affirmations, such as, "You are my beloved daughter in whom I am well pleased." After the blessing is complete, the participants can embrace and receive a special prayer for all the women.

For Father's Day, we referred to the men as "elders" and "youngers." This is the same basic ceremony that the women use. Elders stand first and receive the group's blessings, then the youngers stand and are acknowledged. As an option, there can be two pairs of elders and youngers who perform the shared blessing for the entire group to observe. Follow this with a few minutes of spontaneous affirmation and blessing from the elders to all of the men.

The experience is healing and creates a dynamic sense of community. In our group, some women stood as mothers and daughters; others stood with women they hardly even knew, yet all experienced a lineage and connection at a soul level as women — and sisters — who had struggled to overcome life's challenges. Together they affirmed love and respect for each other and a great pride flowed freely that nourished all from within.

WHO CAN USE THE RITUAL

Families . . . The extended family can use this celebration as a way to honor and give appreciation for each generation. In a family gathering, the blessings can be shared by exchanging partners so that a blessing is given by each of the grand women in the family to each of the younger women. Two family members need to model the process so everyone is clear on what to do.

Spiritual Leaders . . . This is a dynamic addition to the usual Mother's Day or Father's Day celebrations when included in the Sunday worship service or another banquet honoring mothers and fathers.

21
Remarriage Or Anniversary Ceremony

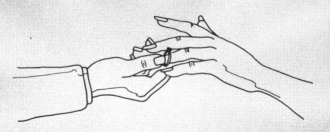

The sacred union of marriage is generally celebrated with great fanfare. Vows of love and commitment for a lifetime are exchanged in front of friends and family. As years pass, couples continue to grow and change. Time needs to be set aside to reaffirm the spirit and commitment of their marriage relationship. The Remarriage Or Anniversary Ceremony is a special rededication and reaffirmation to each other through the renewal of the wedding vows.

YOU'LL NEED

Materials needed are personalized for each ceremony.

THE RITUAL

Use the following suggested outline in a way that fits your specific occasion. Be creative and add as much of your own unique style as possible. There is no right or wrong way to conduct this ceremony, so make it fun and special. The facilitator could be a friend, relative, group leader or member of the clergy.

1. Facilitator welcomes guests and couple to the gathering. A special poem, song or reading may be shared.
2. Invocation prayer or blessing is said by friend or family member. This passage is especially nice:

Blessing For A Marriage

May your marriage bring you all the exquisite excitements a marriage should bring, and may life also grant you patience, tolerance and understanding.

May you always need one another — not so much to fill your emptiness as to help you know your fullness. A mountain needs a valley to be complete; the valley does not make the mountain less but more; and the valley is more a valley because it has a mountain towering over it.

So let it be with you and you.

May you need one another, but not out of weakness.

May you want one another, but not out of lack.

May you entice one another, but not compel one another.

May you embrace one another, but not encircle one another.

May you succeed in all important ways with one another, and not fail in the little graces.

May you look for things to praise, often say, 'I love you!' and take no notice of small faults.

If you have quarrels that push you apart, may both of you hope to have the good sense enough to take the first step back.

May you enter into the mystery which is the awareness of one another's presence — no more physical than spiritual, warm and near when you are side by side and warm and near when you are in separate rooms or even distant cities.

May you have happiness, and may you find it making one another happy.

May you have love, and may you find it loving one another!

Thank You, God, for Your presence here with us and Your blessing on the marriage.

Amen

— James Dillet Freeman

3. Facilitator describes the purpose of the gathering and makes personal comments honoring the couple and their marriage.

4. Family and friends share a special story, song and words of congratulation. The Heart-To-Heart Ritual (see Chapter 2) can be used to facilitate the sharing. A small, red, stuffed heart about six inches across is passed around to everyone and those who want to say something can do so. The heart is then given as a gift to the couples as a symbol of the love that is shared by and with them.

5. Couple shares their thoughts with family, friends and each other. Letters or personal cards can be written in advance and exchanged and read as part of the ceremony.

6. A marriage candle lighting or the exchange of any other symbolic gifts can take place.

7. Facilitator closes with prayer and blessing. All present can join hands and renew their commitment to each other as family and friends.

8. A remarriage or anniversary reception can follow.

Here are some suggestions for the reception:

- Music from the year the couple was wed can be pre-recorded and shared as part of the festivities.
- Family and friends can continue telling favorite stories about the couple's life. These stories can be recorded on video or audio cassettes and kept as special memories.
- Another fun idea is to ask each table of guests to think of a love song and join together as a group and sing or hum it during the meal. Tables are called on one at a time and songs are shared with joy and merriment.

WHO CAN USE THE RITUAL

Families . . . Facilitators chosen from among family and friends can provide the most meaningful stories of the couple's life together. The ceremony honors the couple and community of people around them.

Therapists . . . Couple's groups can use this ceremony as a culminating ritual honoring the participants' growth.

Spiritual Leaders . . . The ritual can be suggested by members of the clergy as a framework to help people design their own personalized ceremony. An annual reaffirmation of relationship for married couples can be held in the Sunday service using a brief ceremony with couples standing together. It can also be a time for those who want to reaffirm their personal relationship with Spirit. Following the service a reception can be held with wedding cake for everyone.

22
Resurrection Ritual

Resurrection means "to rise again." The term commonly applies to the Christian belief that Jesus Christ transcended the death experience to rise into the fullness of eternal life. Our lives also face many challenges, whether they are blows of loss, bondage to fears or the struggle to be our authentic selves. We can face all of our challenges and rise into more abundant life experiences. This ritual uses the format of Jesus' death and resurrection but evokes the universal power within to lift the mind, body and spirit from seeming defeat and loss into the full joy of living in the here and now.

YOU'LL NEED

A group of ten people — larger gatherings can be divided into groups of ten to twelve people.

THE RITUAL

The Resurrection Ritual is adapted from a work done by Bernie Gunther in his book, *What To Do Until The Messiah Comes*. Begin with a brief time of centering, breathing and meditation:

Allow yourself to relax and take a few nice slow deep breaths, focusing the breathing at your heart center.
(Pause)
We have all been hung up on destructive thought patterns, compulsive behaviors, excessive tension or just driving ourselves too hard. Think for just a moment about what these unhealthy actions do to your mind — the effect of continually pushing the body and neglecting the spirit.
(Pause)
When we do this to ourselves, we cut ourselves off from our true feelings; we stop much of the energy and excitement in life. Our body may become uncomfortable, even

painful, to be in. We are pressured and may at times feel exhausted. We can choose to stay in this condition or, with insight and understanding, pull out these "nails" that have us pinned down. We can stop being so hard on ourselves. (Pause)

Let's begin right now to let go of as much of the unnecessary pressure as we are willing to at this point in our lives. (Pause)

Take a quick scan of your body from the inside and begin to acknowledge and let go all the excess body tension. (Pause)

Breathe deep. (Pause)

Be aware of coming off the cross and letting go of your hang-ups. As you allow yourself to come off the cross, realize you are reborn. (Pause)

Realize that you have taken yourself from the cross; you have freed yourself to respond differently to life. The rebirth begins from the inside. Anytime that you feel hung up, you can remind yourself to come off of the cross, let go of the struggle and allow the resurrection to occur again. (Pause)

As you do, you will experience a lighter feeling in your body. Your mind will become more relaxed with a gentle, creative focus. Your spirit is open to experiencing fully the joy that is here in this moment right now. You become more in touch with the excitement of being alive — hearing, seeing, touching, smelling and breathing in the awareness of life. (Pause)

When you are ready, begin to open your eyes. (Pause)

We are going to share together what we have just experienced in our meditation in the Resurrection Ritual. This will all be done in silence. Watch as this group demonstrates.

Be prepared to demonstrate the Resurrection Ritual with a sample group so everyone knows what to expect.

One member of the group of ten lies down, with other members in a circle around them, and thinks of what came to mind in the meditation as a challenging situation or hang-up from which they are willing to begin to be resurrected. Perhaps it is pushing too hard, compulsive behavior, excessive stress or blocking of feelings — whatever that person would like to focus on for the ritual. This will not be spoken or shared with anyone, so make it very personal.

The person lying down should close their eyes, cross their ankles and concentrate on the challenge or hang-up.

The rest of the group uses their fists as hammers and their fingers as nails, and gently applies pressure to the hands and feet of the person on the floor. One person can use her hands as a crown of thorns on the head and apply slight pressure.

Another group member can apply gentle pressure to the chest area with his hands. The pressure should not be forceful or cause discomfort or harm.

As the group applies the nails and pressure, the person on the floor is to imagine the great struggle and pressure of carrying all this. At a certain point the person lets go and symbolically releases the pain and the struggle.

The group members now take out the nails, lift off the crown of thorns and release all pressure. Gently lift and slightly rock the person back and forth for a minute. Be sure to support the person's head. The person can also be rocked in the arms of the group without being lifted.

The group members symbolically use their hands to gently wash the hands and face of the person in the center.

Group members then lay their hands on the person and keep them there for a few minutes while giving a silent affirmation and blessing of love and healing energy. After this is complete, the person in the center takes a few moments to let the whole effect of the experience sink in and then slowly gets up.

The entire experience is re-created for each member of the group.

We have found it helpful to give each group a brief set of steps to follow so that they will remember what to do. Once the first few people have gone through it, the ritual becomes familiar and easy to follow.

Here is a brief outline of the steps:

1. One person lies down, closes eyes and crosses ankles.
2. This person thinks of a challenge or hang-up.
3. Group members use fists as hammers and fingers as nails and gently apply pressure to hands and feet of person on floor.
4. One group member uses their hands as a crown of thorns on the head, and applies slight pressure to head and chest.
5. The person on the floor imagines great struggle and pressure, and then lets go.
6. Group members take out the nails and release pressure.
7. The group members lift or rock the person gently.
8. Group members symbolically wash hands, feet and face of the person.
9. Group members lay hands on the person and keep him there for a few minutes; then group gives the person a silent blessing of love and healing energy.
10. Give the person a few minutes to take in the experience and then repeat this with each person in the group.

WHO CAN USE THE RITUAL

Therapists . . . This is a good ritual for therapists working with groups from a psychospiritual perspective. It can help them to "rise" into an unrestricted way of looking at themselves and their lives, and can help them gain insight and support in their lives.

Spiritual Leaders . . . A powerful ritual used in conjunction with a retreat, or in a group or class setting. Could be used during the seasons of Lent and Easter, but works well independent of the seasonal celebrations.

Recovery Groups . . . Can be used as a hallmark experience of putting to death the old habits and patterns of compulsive behaviors. A memorable experience to initiate or mark any stage of the recovery process.

23
Abundance Ceremony And Check Blessing

ABUNDANCE CEREMONY

For several different reasons, many people have developed negative attitudes toward money. Money may have been a constant reason for fights and threats in the family. Maybe compulsive gambling, inability to save or extreme poverty was a part of one's growing-up experience. Most of us need to develop a more positive relationship with money. We live in an abundant world and money is simply a form of energy that we relate to along with many other life involvements. We can help ourselves by becoming aware of and overcoming negative attitudes toward money, and by entering a more constructive relationship with it — a relationship that is wise, friendly, thankful and positive.

The Abundance Ceremony is a threefold ritual designed to help us better understand our relationship with money by letting a dialogue with money come to us, removing obstacles of lack and limitation and celebrating the abundance of the universe.

YOU'LL NEED

Pencil; paper (or your personal journal); and a loaf or piece of bread.

THE RITUAL

Part 1: Dialogue With Money

Have people sit quietly for a few minutes with their pens and papers. Tell them:

Let thoughts come to you, in a natural, unforced way, of a dialogue with money. Speak to money as if it were a person and let it speak to you. Hear money respond to your thoughts about it. Let money tell you how it operates in your life; let it have a voice so it can speak to you and tell you what it has to say to you so it can help you. Think of money as a friend who wants to relate to you positively and write down its messages to you. Let the dialogue begin.

In a group setting, after the writing has been completed, allow time for sharing with a partner or in small groups. Call people together and ask for a few brief comments from the entire group.

Part 2: Goodbye Letter To Obstacles To Your Abundance

Lead the group in the following meditation:

Become more aware of wanting to let go of the obstacles to your living a more abundant life. Through the dialogue you had with money, you have become aware of some of the attitudes that need to be changed. You are aware of how letting go of some of these attitudes and becoming aware of them is a new beginning to a more prosperous life. You have been so accustomed to these thoughts and beliefs that these obstacles have become a part of your inner landscape, but now you are doing some digging out of entrenched ways of living and clearing them out. You know it's time to say good-bye, so you are going to recognize these obstacles and beliefs and tell them goodbye in a letter. You take the steps toward creating a better relationship with your abundance and realize money is your friend. Money wants to get unblocked in your life. You can begin with: Dear Obstacles, Dear Poverty Attitudes, Dear Lack and Limitation — however you wish to address them. Let the letter begin.

After the letters have been written, the ceremony to honor abundance is held. Each person should have a piece of bread or a loaf may be passed around with each person breaking off a piece.

Part 3: Bread Of Life Abundance Ceremony

Lead the group in this meditation:

Sit quietly for a few moments, relaxing yourself and breathing deeply. Hold the bread in your hands. Fill your mind with all that the bread means, the images it evokes: fields of golden wheat waving gently in the wind; grains of wheat pouring into bins in the flour mill; the smell of fresh-baked bread as it comes out of the oven. Think of the bread and how it is warm; how it is soft on the inside and crisp on the outside.

As you break off a piece of bread, tell the group:

To break bread is a sign of friendship. It is also a sign of abundance, a symbol of nourishment, a symbol of plenty. The bread evokes such similar and individual thoughts in all of us. The bread of life is a symbol shared universally on tables all over the world. It is our bread, full of all that it means to each of us. As we take the bread, we think of our own abundance; reflect on our own prosperity, sharing, giving and receiving. These are the bonds that bind us together. As we hold the piece of bread, we meditate on our bonds to our community — in a common unity — giving and receiving of our prosperity and abundance. Sharing in the abundance of life together, reminding us that there is plenty of everything we all need to sustain us. As we slowly partake of the bread and remember that we are one with the abundance of life, personalize this for yourself: "I am one with the abundance of life."
(Pause)

Chewing slowly — taking in all the essence of all we have shared and will continue to share in our lives each and every day — these new ideas, beliefs and affirmations of abundance become a part of our life, just as the bread becomes a part of our body, an expression of our energy. We give thanks now for our shared abundance and our constant awareness of this, each time we see bread or serve bread or share bread with others.

End the meditation and ceremony by suggesting that the participants write a few positive affirmations concerning their own prosperity and keep them in a prominent place as a reminder of this experience.

WHO CAN USE THE RITUAL

Individuals . . . The Abundance Ceremony can be done as an individual affirmation of one's prosperity. Keeping a personal journal and writing down specific thoughts and feelings after each phase is insightful. Newly acquired awareness can be shared with a family member or trusted friend.

Families . . . Having a family time of sharing about abundance, money and prosperity can create a climate of understanding and mutual support. Celebrating the family's abundance and giving thanks for it is a wonderful way to establish good relationships with money early in children's lives.

Therapists . . . This can be a group experience that helps clients work with valuing themselves and affirming that they deserve to have greater abundance in their lives. It is useful in counseling people with money problems, helping them to learn how to save, spend wisely and get out of debt.

Spiritual Leaders . . . Can be used to help people understand their relationship with God as the source and supply of all things. Can help clarify beliefs about money and spiritual development. Money can be shown as God in action, expressed through us for good purposes.

Teachers . . . This ceremony begins to connect young people with their relationship with money early on and helps identify negative beliefs about money before they become entrenched. Can help children learn to withstand the shallow, unrealistic, materialistic images propagated by the media in order to develop sound personal values and effective money management techniques.

Recovery Groups . . . Money issues are often a great source of frustration leading to stress and relapse. The Abundance Ceremony helps to examine old beliefs and create a more harmonious relationship with one's prosperity. It can also help people identify and counteract compulsive/addictive behaviors concerning money — such as compulsive gambling, credit card abuse and stealing — and contribute to developing wise and healthy uses of money in their lives.

CHECK BLESSING

Since we often deal with money in the form of checks written and received, we affirm a consciousness of wealth and abundance each time we write a personal check by using the Prosperity Stamp. The stamp's inscription, "To give is to recognize how you have received," demonstrates the understanding that to give is to receive. When we use the Prosperity Stamp, we make each experience of writing a check a special honoring of the energy that is being shared, and we reaffirm that the infinte account of All-Good is open for us.

YOU'LL NEED

The Prosperity Stamp (see Appendix B for ordering information)

THE RITUAL

Each time you write a personal check, use the Prosperity Stamp on the front of the check. Place the stamp on the check and think of the beauty of giving and receiving. Look at the hands in its design and contemplate the principle of balance: It is the key to health and prosperity in every area of our lives. As we bless our wealth and allow it to circulate freely, know that we celebrate the natural flow of abundance that surrounds us. And we gratefully draw upon and wisely use this limitless abundance.

WHO CAN USE THIS RITUAL

Individuals . . . The Check Blessing Ritual can transform the ordinary bill-paying experience into an honoring and affirmation of one's personal abundance. It is a stamp of appreciation that creates a positive regard for one's finances.

Families . . . The Check Blessing Ritual can be a time of sharing with the children, allowing them to place the stamp on the front of the checks. A prayer or special blessing can be shared by family members before the monthly bills are mailed.

Therapists . . . The ritual can help to reshape beliefs about money. It can be useful in couple counseling where there are fights, threats or power struggles concerning money.

Spiritual Leaders . . . Many people have had the Bible misquoted to them, believing that "Money is the root of all evil." The ritual can help people understand their relationship with money and clarify beliefs about money and spiritual development. Money can even be seen as a ministry in itself when leaders seek to help people understand that we go where our money goes.

Recovery Groups . . . The ritual provides the physical action of stamping a personal commitment on each check to spend money consciously and wisely. Money once spent on compulsive, addictive habits is now stamped with a symbol of balance and good judgment.

24
Angel®
Cards

Balance

Spontaneity

Birth

Purpose

Adventure

Angel® Cards were developed as a part of The Transformation Game® by Joy Drake and Kathy Tyler for the exploration of consciousness. Along with sample meditations and additional guidelines for their use, each card has a quality of life written on it along with a picture of an angel. The more you think about the quality expressed by the word and picture, the more you will see it reflected in your own life. They are a wonderful way to open or close a group ritual.

YOU'LL NEED

A box of Angel® Cards.

THE RITUAL

Ask each person in the group to close his eyes and select a card. If used as an opening, the group could share what their cards are and what they mean to them personally.

As a closing, cards could be drawn simply as silent blessings. An example of the transformative power of these little cards is shared in the story about "Tom," which follows the Burning Bowl Ceremony.

WHO CAN USE THE RITUAL

Individuals . . . It's fun and inspirational to keep your cards in a small decorative dish on a table where you can receive their love and support on a daily basis.

Families . . . Angel® Cards are a great way to teach children the meaning of new words and introduce them to language used to describe positive qualities of life — words like willingness, tenderness, transformation and inspiration. Exploring these qualities can lead to a powerful experience of them in family life.

Therapists . . . Can be beneficial when used in therapy groups as an opening or closing ritual.

Spiritual Leaders . . . Great for classes, retreats and small groups to help initiate sharing. Can be linked to the fact that angels have acted historically as God's messengers.

Recovery Groups . . . Used in recovery groups, Angel® Cards can become powerful tools for transformation, helping group members focus on and develop the qualities that will lead to positive self-esteem.

25
Rite Of Passage Ritual

Life is a journey full of transitions. We are constantly transforming ourselves into new people. During the growth process, we shed our old behaviors and ways of thinking and don new ones. As we reach these new stages in our development, we often mark the ending of one phase and celebrate our personal passage into a higher level of maturity. These celebrations are called rites of passage.

There are many occasions to commemorate with a rite of passage. Many of the rituals handed down through the ages are examples: baptisms, birthdays, bar/bas mitzvahs, graduations, weddings, anniversaries and funerals.

In the previous chapters of this book, you were given specific guidelines to follow in setting up various transformative rituals. Take the opportunity now to design your own rituals — rituals that will serve as highly personal, conscious celebrations of your uniqueness as a human being in a process of growth and change.

YOU'LL NEED

Whatever props and materials you feel are necessary aids in practicing the ritual.

THE RITUAL

Each rite of passage ritual has three stages: (1) separation or ending; (2) transition, when we are neither the old nor the new; and (3) incorporation or beginning as we move into a new phase. When planning a ritual or ceremony for yourself or someone else, remember these three stages and incorporate them creatively.

WHO CAN USE THE RITUAL

Families . . . Rituals are what help form the fabric of family experience, from large celebrations, such as weddings and holidays, to daily expressions of love and affection, such as kissing each other hello and goodbye. Celebrations of significant family milestones such as birthdays, graduations, honors and awards, job promotions, engagements or births are just a few occasions where rites of passage can be used.

Therapists . . . Rites of passage are wonderful tools for initiating changes in individuals and families. Family dynamics can be analyzed and enhanced through rituals.

Spiritual Leaders . . . Rites of passage are a common part of church ceremony, however, the TR approaches can enhance celebrations of confirmation, invitation, marriage or transition.

Recovery Groups . . . Rites of passage for those recovering from addiction can be used at every step of the process. Participants can use rituals as a way to externalize their inner experiences, marking a rite of passage to a healthy, new beginning, such as the TR experience of the "Empowerment Walk" as a graduation ceremony marking completion of a phase of recovery (see Chapter 12).

TRANSORMATION STORY

When our son, Josh, was about to turn 13, we realized that there were no rituals other than Confirmation in the church to mark this passage into adolescence. Although he did not talk about a ritual, he kept referring to certain death-defying activities that he wanted to try — bungee jumping in particular. Each time he saw a news story about bungee jumping he became excited and made numerous requests to try this sport for his birthday.

Finally, we realized what he meant. He wanted to do something risky in order to create his own rite of passage. Joseph Campbell wrote, "Boys everywhere have a need for rituals marking their passage to manhood. If society does not provide them, they will inevitably invent their own." Josh was asking for something that was an ancient part of his psyche.

David had recently purchased a wonderful pictorial essay called *The Circle Of Life — Rituals From The Human Family*. The chapter on "Initiation And Adolescence" has a vivid picture of Vanuatu teenagers diving from a fifty-foot tower to prove that they are courageous enough to become men. Vines attached to their ankles are just short enough to prevent them from crashing to their deaths. They are the original bungee jumpers!

After many days of reflection, we came up with an idea with which we could all be happy. Our children had loved to sit on our laps and steer the car since the time they were five or six years old. Since the automobile is a symbol of power in our culture, we thought perhaps it would be a good time to let Josh drive the car by himself. Not only would this be a rite of passage for Josh, it would also be one for us. We had to let our son be his own person.

We talked with Josh about the many metaphors of the car. For a long time we had been helping him steer his life; we all had our hands on the wheel. We had told him over the years when to stop and put on the brakes, and when to put on the gas and get moving in his life. Now he would be steering his own life, deciding for himself when to stop or go and in which direction to go.

When Josh's birthday arrived, we told him of our idea. He was excited about driving the car himself. He was also a little nervous. We helped strengthen his confidence by reminding him that all the family would be with him in the car, just as we would remain with him through life — loving, supporting and helping him in any way we could.

When the big evening came, we went to a large, deserted parking lot. Josh drove beautifully by himself. As we watched him drive, we realized that we had to let him go on to the next phase of his life by letting him steer and drive. He seemed to sense some of our deep feelings and said that he would still need us to be around and help him in his life.

This occasion was an important milestone for all of us. The rite of passage was risky enough to fill Josh's need to be daring and master his own life. It empowered him with the sense that he could take charge of his own primal energies and direct them without fear.

Many families could join together to create transformative rites of passage that add to the traditional parties and church services. Creating and participating in these moments together as a family creates a milestone for each person. The unique rites of passage also build traditions that are unique to our time while connecting with our ancient roots.

Appendix A

GUIDELINES FOR PERSONAL TR EXPERIENCE

1. *Keep a personal journal.* Focus on the issue that most concerns you at this time. Write down thoughts and feelings and ask yourself, "What do I long for?" Transformation can come by actively participating in your life, acknowledging the quest for deeper meaning and finding nourishment and support from inner resources. Honor your life and your progress by reading over your journal periodically.

2. *Complement the TR with the appropriate environment.* Each ritual has a focus and some required materials. Choose a time and place that is quiet and free from distractions. You may want to honor the sacred space you are creating with a special prayer, incense, song, music, lighting, clothing, candles, pictures, chimes or other personal means of creating a beginning and ending. Be creative; make it an adventure.

3. *Keep track of your progress.* After you have completed a ritual, go back to your journal and write briefly about any new awareness, insights, shifts in feeling, changes in mood or bodily sensations. You may choose to share some of these insights with a trusted friend, counselor, minister, support group or family member.

4. *Set aside time for play.* As new growth and insight take place in your life, relax the intense inner focus. Allow the unfolding of new awareness to take place within. Reach out to others and volunteer or help someone you know in a way that is meaningful to you.

5. *As you encounter blocks (and we all do), look to see if they are caused by fear.* We often shape our lives in an attempt to avoid what we fear most. Within that fear is all the power you need to change and grow. Through journal writing, discover what is molding your life. Take charge and confront your fears. By doing so you will gain an enormous sense of power and mastery over your own destiny.

6. *Celebrate your new growth.* Mark your change and new insight with a TR celebration. Celebrate your freedom in living. Write a poem, paint a picture, dance, sing, invite others to a ceremonial dinner. Celebrate your life as a masterpiece in progress!

GUIDELINES FOR GROUP TR EXPERIENCE

1. *Let people choose whether to participate.* They can say "yes" or "no" to any TR experience, and no questions should be asked as to why they might not want to do a certain ritual. We very seldom have a situation where a person does not want to participate fully, but it does occur sometimes. Respect the rights and needs of each individual.

2. *Stress group support.* Participation in the rituals gives people the opportunity to share in the power of love. We need to be honest and open with others and with ourselves. If we truly do this, our honesty will be for the purpose of love. Make sure that people aren't just venting their irritations, prejudices or fears.

3. *Stress learning and transformation by doing.* As a facilitator, do what others are doing. In some instances you will need to observe so you can give feedback on what happened; but in other instances, when you *can* have the TR experience, participate fully.

4. *Ask people to speak in the first person when they are talking about themselves.* So often, people talk about themselves in a veiled, unaware fashion. For instance, "When you have been closed up for a long time and are afraid of saying the wrong thing, it's difficult to walk in here and make some big changes." That person is not talking about "you" but about herself or himself. By using "I" when speaking of my experience, I increase the potential for transformative experiences. Remind people of this and notice the change it makes as people "own what they are saying."

5. *Keep people focused on the immediate TR experience they are having in the group.* If they start talking about situations outside of the group, the tendency is for the group to get into advising, taking sides, being preachy or telling how they solve *their* problems. Do not let people stray too far from the here and now. Growth is in the present.

6. *Treat people with love and respect, but be pleasantly firm.* This is a delicate area because you want the group to be active, have "get up and go," and share a certain amount of leadership and spontaneity. At the same time you need to stay on top of things to carry out the TR experience and make sure that all of the people in the group get a chance to participate.

7. *Make sure everyone feels a part of the ceremony and can see and hear well.*
If possible, keep circles fairly small so all can hear. In larger groups, be
sure there is adequate amplification of your voice so everyone hears the
directions.

8. *Start and end the group with some kind of reading, blessing or meditation.*
The opening may be given by you or someone else in the group. You may
want to ask others to participate in this part of the opening ritual process.
The closing at the end of each TR group session can be done by people
just speaking out a word or some thought they have. You may want to
sing at the beginning or end. People may get together in a closing foot-
ball-like huddle or "the spiral." The spiral is a chain of people — joined
together with arms around shoulders or arms linked — standing in a
loose spiral.

SPECIAL THANKS

Illustrations

Thanks to Keith D. Williamson, a graduate of Kansas City Art Institute. He is a freelance designer and four-color computer production specialist in San Antonio, TX. Thanks also to graphic artist Dave Fraser of Artworks Studio, Troy, MI.

Poems

Thanks to Reuben M. Waterman for letting us use his poem in the Burning Bowl Ritual. Our gratitude also to James Dillet Freeman for his poems, "One Step More" and "Blessing For A Marriage," used with permission of Unity School of Christianity, Unity Village, MO 64065.

Special thanks to Leona Stefanko, formerly Unity School of Christianity, for sharing many of these special ceremonies with us.

World Celebration Ceremony

The World Celebration ceremony was created by Sandra Weisner and adapted for use here.

Divorce Ceremony

The Divorce Ceremony was shared with us by Judith A. Grimes in collaboration with other Unity students.

A Walk With God

A Walk With God script was authored by Jim Rosemergy.

Home Blessing

The Home Blessing was adapted from a ceremony written by Theresa Ruhlman.

Appendix B

RESOURCES

The Prosperity Stamp

The Prosperity Stamp was developed by Judith Kemble as a "Fiscal Fitness" tool. It is copyrighted and available from The Art's Desire — TC, P.O. Box 212, Dearborn, MI 48121. Or call (313) 897-2094 for more information. The stamp set, including the rubber stamp and rainbow-colored ink pad, is $12.50 per set plus $1.50 for shipping and handling. Michigan residents add 4% sales tax.

Angel® Cards

Angel® Cards are copyrighted (Drake & Tyler, 1981) and Angel® is a registered trademark. The Angel® Cards were developed as a part of the Transformation Game® by Joy Drake and Kathy Tyler while living at the Findhorn Foundation for the Exploration of Consciousness and may be purchased at many book stores. They are produced by Narada Productions and distributed by Music Design, 1845 North Farewell Avenue, Milwaukee, WI 53202.

Home Blessing And Cleansing Decal

"This House Is Protected By God" decal was created as a visual affirmation and reminder that God is our source of divine protection. Using the six colors of the rainbow, it is a dazzling piece of art that illuminates any window or door in your home (size 3¼" x 3¼"). The decal is available from Things To Be Done, 20001 Greenfield Rd., Detroit, MI 48235. Price: $3.50, plus postage. Quantity discounts available.

Suggested Reading

C.G. Jung, *Collected Works*. Translated by R.F.C. Hull. Edited by Sir Herbert Read, et. al, 20 vols. Bollingen Series XX, Princeton, NJ: Princeton University Press, 1953-1979. XVIII, 625-628.

Eric Butterworth, *The Universe Is Calling*, Harper Collins Publishers, 1993, p. 23

The New Jerusalem Bible, Bantam Doubleday Dell Publishing Group, 1985, pp. 1055-1056.

About The Authors

Gay Williamson, M.A., is a psychotherapist with a degree in clinical and humanistic psychology from the Center for Humanistic Studies in Detroit. Gay has incorporated the use of Transformative Rituals in her private practice and group work as a therapist, in spiritual community, educational settings, in recovery groups and with individuals and families wanting to use rituals and ceremonies creatively for personal growth. Her bachelor's degree in education has opened the way for many children, teens and teachers to be touched in and out of the classroom by her special use of ceremonies, rituals, and rites of passage. She is a retreat/workshop leader, counselor, filmmaker, television producer/host and administrator. Gay expresses her joy and enthusiasm for life by playing her guitar and leading group singing, chanting and transformative meditations.

David Williamson, D.Min., a Unity minister for more than three decades, has made transformative experiences a part of his life and work as a minister, broadcaster, filmmaker, retreat/workshop leader, counselor and administrator. He has a master's degree in educational administration and a doctorate from the prayer- and meditation-based Ecumenical Theological Center in Detroit, where he majored in holistic spirituality and health. He served as senior minister to 6,000 families of Detroit Unity Temple for 18 years. During that time, David wrote, produced and broadcast his own popular self-help radio programs which were carried on a classical music station six days a week for 18 years.

Gay and David Williamson write, speak and present workshops internationally. They are based at The Transformative Center in the Detroit area.

Meditation Tapes
Featuring Gay or David Williamson

Tapes available at $11.50 each, including shipping.

Burning Bowl Ceremony (By Gay)

The Burning Bowl meditation is a symbolic way to cleanse one's life; to mark a rite of passage into a new way of viewing oneself; a New Year's Eve rite of passage; as a process in recovery; as a ceremony of forgiveness and a symbolic way to transcend the past.

Life Symbol Ritual (By David)

The purpose of this meditation is to receive more understanding of one's own purpose, meaning and individual uniquenesss. This is also an effective way to get to know one another center to center.

White Stone Ritual (By David)

The meditation helps to lead one into the awareness and identification of a new spiritual name and inner resources, marking a new beginning in one's life; beginning a new year.

The Phoenix Rising Ritual (By Gay)

The focus of this meditation is to help people gain greater freedom in their life. The Phoenix is a reminder of the winged, transcendent self that rises into new freedom and freshness of life.

Phoenix Medallions:

(Thanks to James Dillet Freeman for the idea of the Phoenix Medallions, which he used in a Silent Unity service.)

The medallions are embossed, silver-colored metal coins, 1½" in diameter, with the Phoenix on one side and blank on the other. Medallions must be ordered in groups of 50 at a cost of $7.50, plus $1.50 shipping and handling.

The Transformative Center
P.O. Box 20010 • Ferndale, MI 48220 • Phone: (313) 342-0878 or Sandra du Monde at (313) 677-1369

Please call or write for detailed brochure.

Books To Set Your
Spirit Free

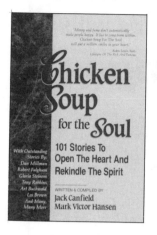

Chicken Soup For The Soul
101 Stories To Open The Heart And Rekindle The Spirit
Jack Canfield and
Mark Victor Hansen

Here is a treasury of 101 stories collected by two of America's best-loved inspirational speakers. Metaphors for life's deep and profound truths, these stories provide models for what is possible, give us permission to be more fully human, and illuminate and clarify the path we walk. Just what the doctor ordered to heal your soul and put a smile on your face.

Code 262X (paperback) $12.00
Code 2913 (cloth) $20.00

Acts Of Kindness
How To Create
A Kindness Revolution
Meladee McCarty and
Hanoch McCarty

The long-overdue kindness revolution is sweeping the country and is waiting for you to enlist! This delightful book tells you everything you need to know to perform intentional acts of kindness for your family, friends, co-workers, schoolmates, strangers and people in need. With ideas and directions for over 100 heartwarming things to do, you'll never run out of ways to spread sunshine.

Code 2956 .... $10.00